A Special Kind of Brain

of related interest

Nonverbal Learning Disabilities at Home
A Parent's Guide
Pamela B. Tanguay
Foreword by Byron P. Rourke, FRSC
ISBN 1 85302 940 8

Nonverbal Learning Disabilities at School
Educating Students with NLD, Asperger Syndrome and Related Conditions
Pamela B. Tanguay
Foreword by Sue Thompson
ISBN 1 85302 941 6

Employment for Individuals with Asperger Syndrome
or Non-Verbal Learning Disability
Stories and Strategies
Yvona Fast and others
ISBN 1 84310 766 X

Relationship Development Intervention with Young Children
Social and Emotional Development Activities for Asperger
Syndrome, Autism, PDD and NLD
Steven E. Gutstein and Rachelle K. Sheely
ISBN 1 84310 714 7

Relationship Development Intervention with Children,
Adolescents and Adults
Social and Emotional Development Activities for Asperger
Syndrome, Autism, PDD and NLD
Steven E. Gutstein and Rachelle K. Sheely
ISBN 1 84310 717 1

Asperger's Syndrome
A Guide for Parents and Professionals
Tony Attwood
Foreword by Lorna Wing
ISBN 1 85302 577 1

A Special Kind of Brain
Living with Nonverbal Learning Disability

Nancy Russell Burger

Foreword by Byron P. Rourke

Jessica Kingsley Publishers
London and Philadelphia

First published in the United Kingdom in 2004
by Jessica Kingsley Publishers
116 Pentonville Road
London N1 9JB, England
and
400 Market Street, Suite 400
Philadelphia, PA 19106, USA

www.jkp.com

Library of Congress Cataloging in Publication Data
A CIP catalog record for this book is available from the Library of Congress

British Library Cataloguing in Publication Data
A CIP catalogue record for this book is available from the British Library

ISBN 1 84310 762 7

Printed and Bound in Great Britain by
Athenaeum Press, Gateshead, Tyne and Wear

This book is dedicated to
My father and my hero
Calvin D. Russell
[3-3-32 to 1-5-04]
Who taught me
How to find my voice,
Who dared me
To be different,
And who encouraged me
To piss in the soup whenever possible.

Contents

Foreword by Byron P. Rourke   9

Introduction   11

1   What's the Matter with Jimmy?   15

2   The Diagnosis and Dealing with It   29

3   At Home: Parenting the NLD Child   44

4   Managing Inflow: The Kid in the Candy Store   58

5   Persever-what?   71

6   Socialization: It's a Jungle Out There   86

7   Teaching Social Skills   98

8   Activities for the NLD Child   112

9   NLD at School: Working with the System   124

10 Discussing NLD with Your Child   144

11 Living with NLD Every Day   156

12 Changes in Routine and Moving—A Four-Letter Word   170

13 Getting Involved   187

14 Seeking Outside Help for Your NLD Child   196

15 Looking Ahead   208

    Epilogue   211

    Acknowledgments   213
    Resources   215
    Bibliography   217
    Index   218

Foreword

The syndrome of Nonverbal Learning Disabilities has been described in detail, and its practical and theoretical implications have been explained (Rourke 1989, 1995a; Rourke, van der Vlugt, and Rourke 2002). But there is a relative scarcity of materials for the parent of the person with NLD (e.g. Rourke 1995b; Tanguay 2001). This book helps to expand this literature.

A Special Kind of Brain is a book all parents of children with NLD should read. It is comprehensive, straightforward, and practical. Much of the important neurological and neuropsychological literature regarding the nature of NLD that can so often be confusing and frustrating for parents to sort through, is clearly and concisely reviewed. In addition, and of principal importance, the implications of these dimensions are spun out in a highly readable manner.

From basic descriptions of how to get things running smoothly on a daily basis to more involved issues such as how to set up an individualized education plan, this book is invaluable in illuminating the challenges children with NLD and their parents may face. The reader is also provided with an abundance of literature, resources, and recommendations regarding how to receive outside support.

Each chapter stands largely on its own, and one could read this book in almost any order. The material presented is easy to understand and readily applicable in a variety of settings. Summaries are provided that can be accessed and used as a quick reference for parents when similar issues with their child arise. Checklists and organizational hints are also supplied to help make sense of meetings and paperwork from schools, physicians, and other sources. How to inquire about issues to ensure that children receive the best services possible to facilitate their style of academic learning and social interaction is also detailed.

The author provides a positive, compassionate, and uplifting perspective on the world of NLD. Her very apt anecdotes are enjoyable as well as informative. The descriptions of Jimmy's exploration of his world, from his fascination with tractors and microwaves to his endeavors to find friendships, provide a constructive glimpse into the remarkable life of a child with NLD. For all parents looking to have their many questions answered, this book will not disappoint. It is highly recommended.

Byron P. Rourke, FRSC
April 2004

References

Rourke, B.P. (1989) *Nonverbal learning disabilities: The syndrome and the model.* New York: Guilford Press.

Rourke, B.P. (1995a) Introduction and overview: The NLD/white matter model. In B.P. Rourke (ed.) *Syndrome of nonverbal learning disabilities: Neurodevelopmental manifestations* (pp.1–26). New York: Guilford Press.

Rourke, B.P. (1995b) *Treatment program for children with NLD.* In B.P. Rourke (ed.) *Syndrome of nonverbal learning disabilities: Neurodevelopmental manifestations* New York: Guilford Press.

Rourke, B.P., van der Vlugt, H., and Rourke, S.B. (2002) *Practice of child-clinical neuropsychology: An introduction.* Lisse, The Netherlands: Swets & Zeitlinger.

Tanguay, P.B. (2001) *Nonverbal learning disabilities at home: A parent's guide.* London: Jessica Kingsley Publishers.

Introduction

Parenthood turns us into living, breathing, fretting magnifying glasses. Everything our child sees, we see more deeply because we were once children ourselves. Every time our child feels pain, we feel it more acutely, simply because we so want to rid them of it all together. When they're happy, we're delirious. When they're sad, we're downtrodden. But when our child struggles with something that the world at large doesn't fully understand and, even worse, tends to fault them for—this is beyond sympathy and/or empathy—in fact, it's far beyond what we have come to expect as parents. This is what *nonverbal learning disability (NLD)* represents to those of us who have watched a child consistently misfire in his world, to become socially isolated and generally misunderstood. Even more frightening is this: such widespread misunderstanding can lead our children to lose the love for themselves that we have tried so earnestly to nurture. How can we protect them from that? The answer is, we can't. But what we can do is manage the world around them by trying to avoid situations that make them feel unsuccessful. While this sounds simple, and what any parent would do, the logistics can sometimes feel impossible. But this is our charge as parents of NLD children and, as difficult as it may seem at first, it eventually becomes as much a part of our daily lives as worrying about whether they'll make the bus or what this week's bully might try on the playground.

This is what I intend to accomplish with this book—to provide a friendly NLD road map, if you will, to help parents, extended family, friends, professionals, and anyone who comes in contact with the NLD child to better understand the ins and outs of this sometimes hard to grasp disability.

My hope is that this book, first of all, will help the many parents of children with NLD to understand that theirs is not a solo mission—that there are other parents struggling with the very same quandaries and heartbreaks they face. If any of the stories or anecdotes outlined herein help this community of parents and children to deal just a little bit better with the difficult issues of friends, family and school, I will have done what I set out to do.

I want to clarify a few points here: First, I'm sure the reader will detect that, throughout this book, I consistently refer to the NLD child in the male/he person. I do this not to insult all of the miraculous girls among my readership (I, too, have a precious daughter) or to be politically incorrect. I do it because my muse in this case happens to be my son Jimmy and it offers some consistency and simplicity in the writing process.

Second, the thrust of this book is the parenting of an NLD child. I therefore refer most often to the caregiver as being a mother or a father. While I have been fortunate to be able to work part time and be home much of the time, I am completely sympathetic to the fact that in many families, both parents work full time. Any of the skills and tips discussed herein can be learned by a caregiver and, with the right fit, a family can work together with such a person so that the dynamic can be smooth and the home environment for the NLD child can be a secure and nurturing one.

I hope that you find this book enjoyable as well as informative. For those of you that may be reading this after just receiving a diagnosis, you may still find yourself in the stage of shock and even grief at learning that your child has nonverbal learning disorder. Please know that, in deciding how to present all of the information that I had to offer, I chose to inject humor here and there, because I think that there are times when living with NLD is just that—funny as heck. But I would not want you to misinterpret my tone as one of flippancy. Life with NLD is a journey which, in my opinion, is best served by acquiring a keen sense of humor. There are many struggles, many victories, and many times when the best thing to do is laugh. There isn't a second when I don't take NLD seriously—I just don't believe we should take ourselves too seriously.

When my son was diagnosed with NLD, my husband Dave and I quite understandably went through a period of panic and excessive worry. As I look back over the last five years, it becomes abundantly clear that the most frightening part of the whole experience was the level of ignorance we suffered at the very outset. So, I resolved to learn every-thing I could in the shortest amount of time. My first stop, of course, was the internet, where I found reams of information, resources, chat rooms and the like—all of which bring me to the second most frightening time. Too much information was not the answer. I spent an evening reading everything available and, when I was through, I was really through. Translated: (a) it is possible to do too much research; (b) the internet, although quite helpful, can be downright frightening when it is used excessively in the absence of professional consultation.

This is certainly not to imply that we won't face our share of disap-pointment, but every child is different and it serves no purpose to spend one's precious time scouring over what-ifs or whipping ourselves into a counterproductive frenzy. After my first ill-advised foray, Dave and I resolved to gather information about the disorder in a more methodical (and less emotional) manner so that we could understand what Jimmy faces and how we can help him now, rather than agonizing about what might happen later. Now, five years later, we have attended as many con-ferences and lectures as possible, all the while ferreting out a number of valuable resources for information and support (a list of which has been included at the end of the book). We have become Jimmy's advocates, and have learned a lot about the disorder and his view of the world because of that work. That is not to say that we don't worry about how Jimmy will function as an adult. Of course we do. But our circle of influence surrounds the here and now and, while what we have estab-lished today may very well help him in the future, our vision for the time being should remain fairly nearsighted.

As my husband so eloquently said to me one particularly dark day, "We can allow ourselves three seconds of self-pity, then we have to just get on with living and with helping Jimmy." This is very true. We must be compassionate enough to understand that feeling bad is okay because NLD is not fun for us or for our kids. We're not supposed to be pleased with the struggles and challenges that we face individually or as a family. But there's really no time or purpose in wishing it weren't a part of our lives. There are myriad methods of parenting, schooling, and socializing in an effort to make the NLD child more comfortable in his skin and in his world, and we must work toward implementing them in every way we can. Most importantly, we must never lose sight of the fact that NLD children, like all children, need to be loved and accepted for who they are. And, as parents, we should not make the mistake of becoming overzealous in our efforts to teach them how to compensate for their deficiencies. Like everything else, there is a time for work and a time for play. The NLD child is not in need of repair, but of patience, tolerance, acceptance and, *always*, of love and affection. These children are not projects, but rather miracles whose differences make them unique and wonderful—and they must be given the chance to shine in their own special way.

Nancy Russell Burger
April 2004

Chapter 1

What's the Matter with Jimmy?

I am large. I contain multitudes.

Walt Whitman, Leaves of Grass

As a child, the most difficult thought I could fathom was the idea of something being wrong with either of my parents. Now, as a parent myself, there is nothing more excruciating than the thought of something being wrong with either of my own children. On this I think all parents can agree, and once those few first moments after childbirth elapse and the neonatologist gives you the high sign, you breathe the deepest sigh of relief. Now, if you can just get through the rest of his life, you say to yourself, everything should be all right...

According to most of us who watched Jimmy wander off into the depths of our backyard during his third birthday party (ignoring the 16 or so guests clamoring to get into the ball pit or the jungle gym), he "marched to a different drummer." While exceptionally well spoken for a child of his age, he couldn't relate to his peer group and quickly lost interest in what others would say to him, often looking off into space or interjecting comments completely unrelated to the conversation at hand. From the age of two, he tended toward fixation, his first being on the microwave, the next on the musician James Taylor. He would watch Mr. Taylor's videos and listen to audio tapes until every detail was committed to memory, and for a time Jimmy insisted on dressing only—and I mean only—in one particular outfit similar to one he saw the musician wear during a concert (I found myself laundering a pair of khakis and a blue shirt almost daily). Jimmy practiced holding his toy guitar in precisely the same way as the minstrel himself, and memorized not only all of JT's song lyrics but also the names of his band members and their instruments with obsessive accuracy. As parents, Dave and I felt this was all a bit over the top, but we tried to find some humor in it and allowed that it was indicative of an extremely active and creative mind.

At age three, Jimmy became enthralled with lawn tractors, trimmers and blowers; a particularly problematic fixation since he was also petrified of the sounds they made. This fear would cause him to run circles around the house at the mere mention of cutting the grass. Once the mower actually started up, our poor son would sob and sweat, begging us to close all windows and doors notwithstanding the 90-degree heat. It was a terrible struggle for him to fear the very thing that obsessed him the most and we had to prepare him for days ahead of time when the grass was going to be cut. I would try to reassure him with hugs, but he needed to be running around in circles or the hysteria would only escalate. There were some days when, as a preemptive measure, I would gather everyone in the van and take a trip to the park or the grocery store a good half hour before our lawn service people were expected—and then have to play dumb upon returning home to a freshly cut lawn.

Jimmy was our firstborn, so as far as we were concerned these travails were all grist in the parenthood mill. We had, after all, no barometer, no point of comparison except for other toddlers of Jimmy's age, with whom he had only occasional contact. While I did arrange for play dates with other children, these usually resulted in parallel play (which was age appropriate and therefore threw up no red flags to us) with mothers attempting to socialize while chasing their urchins from one room to the next. Dave and I accepted Jimmy's behaviors as idiosyncratic, but nothing to be overly concerned with. In reality, these behaviors were an early introduction to a syndrome called *nonverbal learning disability*, or *NLD*.

What is NLD?

Nonverbal learning disability is defined as a dysfunction of the brain's right hemisphere—that part of the brain which processes nonverbal, performance-based information, including visual—spatial, intuitive, organizational and evaluative processing functions (Rourke 1995). Contrary to what the name implies, children with nonverbal learning disability are anything but nonverbal. In fact, one of the great strengths of these children is their ability to verbally express themselves. This is so strong, in fact, that often the child is considered exceptionally bright and gifted at a very young age. Of course, I am not suggesting that this is never the case. However, it is also symptomatic of the disability.

Okay, so what does this mean to us parents? Well, since the right hemisphere governs the abstract, intuitive functions of the brain, and since much of what goes on in daily life is, well, pretty abstract, it should come as no surprise that, to the NLD child, the world at large is a chaotic, confusing place which is difficult to break down into meaningful parts.

NLD was first discovered in the early 1970s through the study of learning disabled children who showed notable discrepancies between their verbal and nonverbal IQ scores. The preeminent researcher in the field of NLD is Dr. Byron P. Rourke of the University of Windsor, Canada, and Yale University. After decades of research, Dr. Rourke and his associates have determined that NLD is caused by damage to the white matter in the brain—the tiny highways that carry information, nerve impulses and the like from one region of the brain to another. Dr. Rourke refers to this theory as his "White Matter Model" (1995).

There are, in fact, three distinct types of white matter in our brains: we'll call them right/left fibers (corpus collosum); back/front (arcuate) fibers; and up/down (projection) fibers. I'm certainly no neuroscientist, but I'll try to explain the differences between these fibers in fairly simple terms:

1. *Right/left fibers:* these connect the brain across the midline— that is, they connect similar sections of the right and left hemispheres of the brain.

2. *Back/front (arcuate) fibers:* these connect different sections of the same hemisphere of the brain.

3. *Up/down (projection) fibers:* these essentially "shoot" information up and down from the hemispheres to the brain stem, spinal cord and back.

According to Dr. Rourke's theory, in order for NLD to occur there must be damage to the right/left fibers of the brain (the corpus collosum)— that is, those "highways" that transport information between the right and left hemispheres of the brain. The main theoretical principles and conclusions of Dr. Rourke's White Matter Model are summarized as follows:

- In general, the more white matter (relative to total brain mass) that is abnormal, removed, or dysfunctional, the more likely it is that the NLD syndrome will be in evidence.

- Which white matter is abnormal, removed, or dysfunctional and at which stage of development this occurs have an important bearing on the manifestations of the NLD syndrome.

- Right hemisphere white matter is crucial for the development and maintenance of its specific functions, such as intermodal integration (being able to process visual and auditory information simultaneously), especially when new information processing situations are encountered.

- Left hemisphere white matter is essential for the development but not necessarily the maintenance of its specific tendencies. For example, certain linguistic skills are often found to remain intact after significant damage to the left cerebral hemisphere in adults.

The theoretical principles outlined above lead to the following deductions:

- A significant abnormality confined to the right cerebral hemisphere may constitute a sufficient condition for the production of the NLD syndrome.

- The necessary condition for the presentation of the NLD syndrome is the destruction or dysfunction of white matter that is required for intermodal integration. (Rourke 1995)

What causes this damage? Well, that's the sixty-four million dollar question that no one has yet been able to answer. It could be that there is a genetic component to NLD. Growing up in Dutchess County, New York, with one older sister, I was a late bloomer myself. I wasn't even five years old when they pried me off of my mother's leg and shoved me onto the kindergarten bus. My dad worked for IBM and my mom was a homemaker. I attended college in upstate New York and went to work in Manhattan for 11 years, married Dave and made my way to Connecticut where we have settled. I'm a mother, a writer and a musician (vocalist for a band called Gravel Road). Dave was late to reach puberty as well, and spent much of his young life playing basketball and football and building model airplanes. He grew up in Westchester County, New York, with two older sisters, graduated from Fredonia College in upstate New York and spent many years in financial jobs in Manhattan before joining GE Capital in Stamford, Connecticut. Both Dave and I had struggles in elementary school and social difficulties as children. However, it's easy to witch hunt when you have the advantage of a 20/20 rear view mirror, especially when it would be such a huge relief to find an answer to such a burning question as where in the blazes did this NLD come from?

Another theory—one which we both find exceedingly more disturbing—centers on the question of childhood immunizations. While I will preface this by saying that there is currently *no conclusive evidence* which links childhood immunizations to learning disabilities or neurological disorders, in the year 2000 the Institute of Medicine (IOM)[1] did a study which focused on the safety of the existing immunization program for children. Specifically, the study focused on what, if any, was the nature of the relationship between the presence of the mercury-based preservative thimerosal in vaccines and the neurodevelopmental disorders of autism, attention deficit hyperactivity disorder (ADHD) and speech or language delay in children.

The results of the IOM study were pretty inconclusive. They stated that the evidence was "inadequate to accept or reject" a relationship between exposure to thimerosal from vaccines and autism, ADHD and speech and language delay. However, the study went on to state that, although a direct relationship between the exposure to thimerosal and these disorders could not be established, the "hypothesis is biologically plausible." What does all of this *mean*? While the study found no concrete, conclusive evidence that thimerosal leads to autism, ADHD and speech and language delay in children, we can't rule it out.

I have had the pleasure of meeting Dr. Rourke, and am honored that he wrote the Foreword to this book. In fact, Dave and I brought Jimmy to his office in Windsor, Ontario, in 2001 for a complete evaluation. It was a fascinating and wonderful experience for all of us, and we found Dr. Rourke to be not only brilliant, but exceedingly kind, helpful and supportive on a very human level. Most importantly, he confirmed the diagnosis of NLD (which we had received in 1999 at the Connecticut Children's Medical Center in Newington), and gave us a great deal of moral support and inspiration to continue steadfastly on our course—to keep "doing what you are doing." This is something that all parents of NLD children truly need—validation and confirmation that they are on the right track. We didn't necessarily think we weren't, but we also weren't sure we were. It was not a risk we were willing to take with our son.

How common is NLD?

According to some statistics provided by the US Department of Education's Office of Special Education Annual Report (1999), 12.8 percent of all children enrolled in school in the US are in special education, and over 8 percent of the children enrolled in school in the US are specifically qualified for special education in the areas of learning disabilities and speech and language impairment—two areas where NLD children are identified. According to Dr. Byron Rourke, 10 percent of the children in learning disordered populations have NLD, which would indicate that about 1 percent of the general population of the US, or about 2.7 million people, currently have NLD. There seems to be no difference in incidence between girls and boys (Stewart 2002).

Manifestations, or what NLD looks like

How does NLD show up in a child? Basically, there are three different areas that are affected by the disorder: *motoric, visual—spatial,* and *social.* However, as with any disorder, it is important to understand that not *all* of the areas described below will necessarily prove problematic in all NLD children.

Motoric

An NLD child will often appear clumsy and trip or knock over things quite regularly. This is because he is usually weak in both fine and gross motor skills. Riding a bike will present a challenge because of all of the skills that must be intertwined—pedaling, keeping balance, looking forward; this is a lot for an NLD child to do all at once and may be an exercise in frustration. On the fine motor side of the spectrum, using scissors is exceedingly difficult for the NLD child, as is holding a pencil or using an eating utensil properly. Jimmy still becomes frustrated at shoe tying, so he wears Velcro or slip-on sneakers instead. There is no point whatsoever in raising the level of frustration that your NLD child already deals with. Where you can simplify, do it. Also, occupational therapy can help in these areas, and Jimmy's weekly sessions with an occupational therapist improved his strength considerably. Still, parents must be sensitive to the fact that these are areas of difficulty.

Organizational/visual—spatial

Jimmy would give a blank stare whenever I asked him to do a series of tasks—tasks which, to a neurologically typical child, would be fairly simple to execute, such as "Put down your truck, get your coat and hat from the hook and put them on." I was convinced at the time that my child was simply ignoring my directions, being defiant. Nothing could have been less true. He was actually trying to sort out the different things I had asked him to do but, unfortunately, was overwhelmed by the multitask instruction. First of all, NLD children have a lot of difficulty transitioning from one activity to another. So, asking him to put down his truck and stop playing to do something else was the first stumbling block. Next, after asking him to transition, I requested that he do not one thing, but a whopping three: get his coat, get his hat, and then put them both on. The directions confused him and the confusion frustrated him. The result: a blank stare. Worst of all, I might have verbally reprimanded him for not "listening," which only raised the level of stress further. In fact, he was using all of his available energy to "listen" but couldn't sort out what he was supposed to do. He wanted to please me, which only made matters worse for him.

Here are some other "red flags" which got our attention. In preschool, it became apparent that Jimmy did not participate in group activities. At story time in school, for example, he would often lie on the floor, humming to himself. It would help marginally if he were placed in a chair next to the reader, but not always. At first, this seemed to be a gross motor issue: that is, weakness in his torso was making it difficult for him to sit up and pay attention, so he would simply lie down. To alleviate this, we purchased a supportive folding seat (called a "Back Jack") which could be placed on the floor to give him more comfort, but this did not help significantly. Once the NLD diagnosis was delivered, we understood that Jimmy was actually missing all of the social cues that were going on around him. He couldn't focus on the reading of the story, nor could he understand the concept of "personal space" or realize that his humming might disturb others in the group. He was using an enormous amount of energy simply to sit or lie there, trying to sort out the seemingly chaotic environment he found himself in.

The confusion experienced by the NLD child leads to other unusual behaviors. Any situation which is new or unknown to this child will cause a high degree of anxiety. NLD children are easily overwhelmed by visual stimuli, so a busy party or shopping mall can cause them to become quite agitated. When put in these situations, the NLD child may attach himself to an adult to gain a sense of stability and security amid the chaos. Further, the child will try to verbally label everything that he sees and everything that is happening around him through what may seem like an endless monologue. Goodness knows an adult will be infinitely more patient with this behavior than will another child. While some may consider this an attempt by the NLD child to get attention from the adult (which it is, in a way, but not in quite the same way they mean), it is really the child's attempt to hang on to a lifeboat in what seems to be a very choppy sea.

Social

The third and perhaps most disturbing manifestation of NLD is in its social manifestations—that is, the child's difficulty interacting with his peer group. This occurs because the NLD child is unable to pick up nonverbal cues in his environment. When you consider that approximately 65 percent of an average conversation is communicated nonverbally (Thompson 1997), you might understand how difficult it could be for the NLD child, who will try to communicate solely through processing the remaining 35 percent of verbal information he receives. In many cases, he really does not understand what is happening or what is being communicated to him, and the resulting social "misfires" leave him looking inappropriate and awkward.

For instance, if someone is telling you a rather long story and you suddenly look at your watch, that person will get the idea that you're in a bit of a hurry and that they should finish the story fairly soon. A similar cue from a younger person might be even more blatant, like the dramatic rolling of his eyes or his abruptly walking away. Well, the NLD child will not understand these cues, no matter how blatant they are, and will keep on telling the long story to the point where he might even follow the other child as he/she walks away. It isn't difficult to see how this might be irritating behavior to a peer, and may even result in the NLD child being teased and/or excluded from social situations. The irony of this is that the NLD child is desperately trying to fit in, but his actions may be misinterpreted as being impertinent or annoying by both children and adults. The NLD child wants to do the right thing, but often blunders because he simply cannot "translate" the social situations that he finds himself in. Since adults are more polite about this behavior in general, NLD children often feel more comfortable speaking to adults, but this can lead to overdependence, particularly on parents or other caregivers. The lack of interaction with peers only exacerbates the awkwardness in these types of situations.

Black and white, but no gray

For Jimmy, as with most NLD children, what he *hears* is what he *learns*. In order to communicate calmly and effectively with an NLD child, you must put aside innuendo, sarcasm, figures of speech and facetiousness. These parts of language, which most of us have come to know only too well and use regularly, are completely lost on an NLD child and, worse, are confusing and disrupting to him. These children approach the world quite literally and logically so, as parents, we must adjust our way of speaking.

Once, when Jimmy was four years old, his expression turned to horror at my asking him to "keep an eye on" his little sister. To his literal way of thinking, he was being asked to remove an eye from his head and put it on her, an idea that was far too upsetting to be applicable in any way or even remotely funny. Since this was still early on in our family's NLD journey, it took me a minute to realize what Jimmy had heard but, when I did, I quickly rephrased by requesting him to "please watch your sister to make sure she doesn't hurt herself." He was immediately, and understandably, relieved. It was then that I started to appreciate just how different, and sometimes scary, the world really was for my son.

Similarly, when asking an NLD child a question, expect that he will answer *the question that you ask*, not the question that you imply—which pretty much rules out rhetoric as an effective tool of language. We must then take this one step further. Consider the following scenario: NLD child is encountered drying the wet dog with a clean pillowcase. In an irritated tone, mother asks child, "What on earth do you think you're doing?" While normally it would be considered impudent for the child to respond by saying, "I'm drying the dog with my pillowcase," in the case of an NLD child, it is most likely what will happen. The fact of the matter is, the NLD child will give us the very information we request—whether we request it rhetorically or not simply does not factor into his response.

A better way for a parent to handle this situation might be to say "Please stop. I don't want you to dry the dog with a clean pillowcase. Please use an old towel, and remember to not do this again next time."

Other trouble areas

Some other areas of difficulty for NLD children include adaptation to change and lack of discovery learning.

Adapting to change

The parent of an NLD child must take considerable care when dealing with that child's routine. Any change should be introduced well in advance, and every effort should be exerted to avoid last-minute shifts in schedule, etc. These changes put the NLD child's already confusing world in a tailspin. These are not children that can go with the flow. While they will have to adapt to the world around them to a certain degree, we can try to reduce stress by smoothing the rough spots as much as possible.

Lack of discovery learning

Whereas a neurologically typical (NT) child will integrate visual, tactile and auditory experiences to form corresponding concepts and principles, the NLD child learns nothing through discovery. He acquires a great deal of knowledge, however, through his collection of verbal experiences. This was explained quite succinctly and effectively to us with regard to Jimmy in the following way: "If he isn't talking, he isn't learning." This became a kind of mantra for me on those days when I developed a throbbing pain at the base of my skull from my son's incessant jabbering.

Consider these two contrasting scenarios. A neurologically typical toddler might enter someone's living room and look around at all the interesting and colorful knickknacks, picture frames, etc. Once her parent is distracted, the toddler might spot a particularly colorful vase on a table across the room, rise to her feet and scramble over to it, pick it up, feel it, then throw it on the floor. As it crashes to pieces, the toddler's parent shrieks, perhaps takes hold of the child's arm abruptly, reprimands her, and tells her to never touch another thing in that room.

Now let's look at the NLD child in a similar situation: While sitting with his parent, he sees the colorful vase across the room but makes no effort to go to it. He points to it and asks his parent what it is. Once the question is answered, the child pays no more attention to the vase because he has received the information he asked for. Instead, he begins to ask more questions about other objects in the room, and the parent answers with more verbal information.

The difference between these two examples is pretty clear. The typical child sees something she wants to investigate and moves her body toward it. In the process, she keeps her sights on the target all the time and, when she gets close enough, she touches it, lifts it and drops it. She then hears the shout of her parent and feels the shame of the reprimand. This chain of events has resulted in her being exposed to the following notions: a sense of accomplishment and confidence at sighting the object and moving herself to get it, learning the feeling and weight associated with an object of that type, the effect of gravity on an object when released in the air and, last but not least, the consequences of pulling that kind of stunt in front of mom or dad. The NLD child, however, is given the name of the object that he sees, namely a "vase," but nothing else whatsoever is taken away from the experience. He would have to ask at least 15 or so more questions to learn what the other child learned from the activity.

Misdiagnosis

While NLD is becoming more understood with time, it is still a lesser known disorder than many others. As an unfortunate result, many children are left undiagnosed or misdiagnosed. Because of their difficulty focusing on tasks and their inability to learn visually, they are often thought to have Attention Deficit Disorder (ADD) or Attention Deficit Hyperactivity Disorder (ADHD). Clearly, it is essential that the proper diagnosis is obtained, and a good clinician will be able to discern between these disorders.

Possible signs of NLD

The following observations by a teacher may indicate that there is some kind of nonverbal learning deficit, and further evaluation should be pursued by the parent:

- the left margin of the child's work tends to slope to the right and become increasingly wider

- the child becomes confused by multistep directions

- diagonals are difficult for the child to perceive

- the child becomes distressed when asked to copy from a board to paper.

The gift of NLD

When you stop to think about all the aspects of daily life that a typical brain routinely manages, and then consider these same aspects of life given the challenges faced by the NLD child, it isn't difficult to appreciate that these children are often plagued by anxiety. They really can't find order in their universe, and they spend an awful lot of time and energy trying to find it. It's as if your sorted sock drawer was constantly being dumped out and mismatched. But these kids can't give up and wear sandals—and as parents we have to help them make sense out of the socks they've got. Maybe it's also our job to tell them that having a perfectly organized sock drawer isn't always the most important thing after all.

Sometimes, in the early morning, when I am supposed to be waking up my son for school, I find myself watching him sleep, staring at him, really. I marvel at the beauty of his form, the perfection of his head, his face, and I wonder what is happening inside his brain that makes him see things just a little bit differently, what gives him his special perspective on the world, his tireless hunger for detail, his phenomenal memory. There are so many gifts, so many miracles that happen day to day, and I cherish them. It happens with all of our children in the course of a life, yes. But perhaps it's a little bit different with the NLD child because these "gifts"—fixations, endless monologues, impulsivity, to name a few—are initially viewed by parents, myself included, as problem areas difficult for the neurologically typical world to grasp or accept. But gradually, as we grow with our child and begin to see the world through his eyes, we also begin to see how these coping mechanisms represent a unique and masterful way of surviving in an ever-challenging, chaotic world. How wonderful for them that these mechanisms exist, that our ingenious children have found ways to compensate for the manner in which their brains function. Sure, it makes things tough at the lunch table, but I'm convinced that, if it wasn't Jimmy's fascination with James Taylor or lawn tractors, the kid who wanted to bully him in second grade would have found something else to bully him about. Please don't mistake this for rationalization, because if you think I would have chosen NLD for my son, think again. On the other hand, if you think I would change a hair on his exquisite head at this very moment, then I've misrepresented myself. To take the NLD away from my son would be like removing something precious from the ecosystem: you don't know what else it would affect. It reminds me of a scene from the movie *Bruce Almighty*. Once Jim Carrey's character assumed God's powers, he wanted to impress his girlfriend, so he pulled the moon in close to his apartment so he could have the benefit of a huge, full moon as a romantic backdrop. The next day, there were floods and monsoons, death and destruction all over the world because of his childish stunt. Perhaps I'm making my point in a bit of a clumsy way, but you get the idea.

Summary

1. Nonverbal learning disorder is defined as a dysfunction of the brain's right hemisphere—that part of the brain which processes nonverbal, performance-based information, including visual—spatial, intuitive, organizational and evaluative processing functions.

2. The leading authority in the field is Dr. Byron P. Rourke who, through decades of research, has determined that NLD is caused by damage to the brain's white matter, the tiny highways that carry information between the right and left hemispheres of the brain.

3. There may be a genetic component to NLD, but there is also some conjecture as to whether childhood immunizations containing the mercury-based preservative thimerosal may play a role in the onset of this disorder.

4.   There are basically three different areas affected by NLD: motoric, visual—spatial and social, the latter being perhaps the most disturbing and difficult to handle for some parents.

5.   Most NLD children learn what they hear. In order to communicate effectively with them, you must put aside sarcasm and innuendo and stick to literal forms of speech.

6.   Other trouble areas for the NLD child include adapting to change and a lack of discovery learning.

7.   Since the NLD is still a lesser known disorder than many others, many children are left undiagnosed or misdiagnosed.

8.   The NLD child possesses many gifts.

Note

1   The Institute of Medicine was chartered in 1970 by the National Academy of Sciences to "enlist distinguished members of the appropriate professions in the examination of policy matters pertaining to the health of the public." The IOM acts under the Academy's 1863 congressional charter responsibility to be an adviser to the federal government and also initiate the identification of issues of medical care, research and education (NVIC-IOM Vaccine Safety Research and Reports).

Chapter 2

The Diagnosis and Dealing with It

In times of stress, the best thing we can do for each other is to listen with our ears and our hearts and to be assured that our questions are just as important as our answers.

Fred Rogers

When Jimmy started preschool at the age of three, he suffered what we thought was the normal amount of anxiety about being left with a new group of people. At the end of the school year, however, we were shocked to learn that his teachers were "concerned" about his behavior in the classroom. They reported that Jimmy never participated with the group in story time or activities, and often walked off by himself to a corner of the room or looked out the window, apparently waiting anxiously to be picked up. He had to be given instructions several times before he seemed to understand, and he had a lot of trouble with any type of multitask instruction (such as "pick up the blocks and put them in the bin"). They also expressed some concern about the level of fear that Jimmy displayed towards lawn equipment noises. In fact, I was once called to pick him up when he crumbled into sobs at the sight of the lawn maintenance men arriving on school property for their weekly chores.

Jimmy's teachers suggested that I have him evaluated by a psychologist assigned by the public school system in our town. Needless to say, I was as stunned by this suggestion as any parent would be. "What could they possibly mean? Jimmy is a healthy, active three-year-old. He speaks better than most children his age and has a wonderful vocabulary. So he's afraid of loud noises and gets a little infatuated with things. So what? Maybe he's just a bit eccentric." These feelings were, of course, strenuously supported by friends and family who insisted that Jimmy was a genius and simply bored with the activities preschool offered. While not wanting to ignore the teacher's suggestions, we certainly didn't want the public school to tag our son and/or have his psychological profile on file. So, we hired a private child psychologist to evaluate Jimmy in his preschool classroom.

After spending close to an hour watching him, the psychologist concluded that Jimmy displayed a normal amount of separation anxiety while at school, but that she witnessed no "red flags" that would indicate emotional or other problems. She did mention, however, that he seemed a bit clumsy and awkward, and suggested that he be evaluated by an *occupational therapist* with regard to gross and fine motor strength. We did this immediately, and were told that Jimmy suffered from extremely low motor control and strength. We then began a weekly regimen of occupational therapy sessions that were difficult and tiring for Jimmy, but which at least made us feel that we were on the right track toward helping him through his difficulties.

What a relief. It wasn't that our son had any serious problems, we reasoned. Jimmy was just using so much energy to sit still (which took a lot of upper body strength) and to keep straight and balanced that there was not much left over for paying attention to a story or to a group activity. It sounded like a fine explanation, and no one seemed to argue, so we stuck with it. We worked with Jimmy diligently on all the exercises his therapist suggested, and praised him for every effort. We purchased a special seat (the "Back Jack" mentioned in Chapter 1) to place on the floor at school so that his back would be supported at story time—to prevent him from lying on the floor as he always did. We had wheelbarrow races (we would hold Jimmy's legs as he used his arms to waddle throughout the house) and did push-ups with him. It was easy to convince ourselves that, once we helped him strengthen his body, the rest would work itself out. We would fix everything.

Well, the therapy did help his upper body strength, but it wasn't the panacea that we hoped it would be, and Jimmy's struggles continued notwithstanding his now stronger torso and finger grip. Eventually, I became frustrated with the preschool teachers who seemed to offer no more productive input, and we eventually moved Jimmy to a Montessori school. The director there assured me that the school's philosophy embraced children with all learning styles and further emphasized that each student must be allowed to learn at his own pace. Differences were viewed as just that—differences—rather than problems or deviations from some arbitrary notion of normalcy. I left feeling confident and peaceful, looking forward to a new start for my son.

Jimmy thus began in the Montessori program for four-year-olds, and seemed to enjoy his time there. He continued to wander in the classroom with limited attention, but his teachers were fully aware of the occupational therapy he was receiving and took great pains to accommodate by allowing him to sit next to them during story time and to be seated in his special chair (as opposed to the floor) for more support and comfort. Still, by the end of the year, our conference with his teacher, although very positive in certain areas, left us feeling that Jimmy was still suffering in his socialization skills. In fact, he was picked on by some of the other students, and was rarely asked to play dates or birthday parties. Although it probably would have been easy to attribute this to his motor weaknesses or his immaturity, deep down we knew that this was only part of the story. We knew we were missing a bigger picture, that there was something very wrong, and it was time we found out exactly what it was.

Where to go for an evaluation

At the end of the school year, I called Jimmy's pediatrician and discussed our concerns. He immediately referred us to the Connecticut Children's Medical Center (CCMC, which has locations in Hartford and Newington, CT). I contacted them right away and scheduled an "intake" meeting, where we would sit with a member of the staff and discuss the situation so that they could better understand what types of evaluations would be necessary. We would also discuss the cost, insurance issues, and other important topics. After the intake meeting, the evaluation date was scheduled wherein two different specialists would spend time with Jimmy separately to determine where his difficulties were based and what, if any, diagnosis could be ascertained.

Jimmy spent about an hour with an educational specialist and nearly two hours with a child psychologist at CCMC. The evaluations were handled in a very stress-free manner with a lot of play and casual conversation. About a month later, we received by mail a very thorough, written report containing the following: (a) diagnostic perceptual/cognitive assessment; and (b) psychological evaluation. Excerpts from those reports are provided below:

Diagnostic perceptual/cognitive assessment

Jimmy presented as an engaging 4+10 [year+month] year old. He readily accompanied the examiner and his mother to the testing room. Jimmy eagerly engaged in conversation. His language skills on informal measures were satisfactory. He maintained joint attention, conversing appropriately. Jimmy spoke in full sentences and his speech was clear. On formal test measures, Jimmy demonstrated age appropriate linguistic skills…and performed capably on more complex language-based tasks, solving opposite analogies and defining familiar nouns and verbs.

Within this one-to-one setting, Jimmy exhibited significant attention concerns. He required ongoing prompting and verbal cueing to complete presented activities. He was notably physically restless and at one point fell out of his chair. Jimmy's attention issues impeded his performance on memory tasks, both visual and auditory... Weaknesses were evident within Jimmy's perceptual—motor skills, and he had difficulty on paper/pencil tasks. He wrapped four fingers around the pencil, gripping somewhat high on the pencil shaft. His figure drawing was also somewhat primitive, with few discrete parts.

Jimmy's acquisition of basic developmental and readiness skills was largely satisfactory. He demonstrated literary awareness as he opened a book and turned pages appropriately... Jimmy's quantitative skills were age appropriate, and he displayed satisfactory acquisition of basic development conceptual skills... His acquisition of long-term retrieval of information was largely appropriate.

In summary, Jimmy presents as an engaging child who displays variability within his profile. Strengths are evident in language and acquisition of basic readiness concepts and skills. However, notable weaknesses are apparent in his visual perceptual—motor abilities. Concurrently, Jimmy exhibits significant attentional issues which further exacerbate his learning difficulties and reduce his availability to learn; however, his attentional discontinuity does not meet strict criteria for a diagnosis of Attention-Deficit/Hyperactivity Disorder at this time... Jimmy presents a profile of a student with features of a *Nonverbal Learning Disability* as well as significant attentional issues.

Psychological/behavioral observations

James impressed as a likeable, pleasant youngster, one who seemed to enjoy engaging the examiner in conversation. His attention during the assessment period was intermittent, and his lack of attention span appeared to adversely affect his performance. On occasion, he lacked persistence in his problem-solving efforts.

His responses to verbal questions were usually rapid, though accurate. However, with hands-on, visual perceptual—motor tasks, his problem solving was much less rapid and effective. On such tasks, he appeared to lack cognitive flexibility, utilizing the same strategy repeatedly, even when it was clearly unsuccessful.

... The results of the present evaluation reveal a significant discrepancy between James' verbal abilities and his non-verbal, visual perceptual—motor functioning. In general, his verbal abilities are in the above average range, while his visual spatial—motor abilities are in the low average to borderline range. Thus, he best demonstrates his intelligence through the use of verbal skills.

James demonstrated very good development in his acquisition of words and understanding their usage, and appears capable of understanding on a level comparable to that of a somewhat older child. While his vocabulary and verbal reasoning skills appear to be areas of strength, his social reasoning and judgment appear to be relatively weaker. He appears to be more cognizant of the function of objects in his environment and less aware of social, interpersonal information.

Visual—spatial awareness and coordination were deficient, however. James' performance on tasks which tapped these abilities was significantly below his age level...

ADAPTIVE FUNCTIONING

... James attempts to make friends, but is frequently rejected by other children. Furthermore, he is the frequent target of aggression from other children. In play activities that require more than one person, he has not yet developed skills. He is unable to play card or board games, and/or follow the rules of such games. He has not developed group participation skills. Thus, playing with others is a problematic area. Despite his difficulties with others, James is responsible, polite, can control his impulses, and can apologize when he makes mistakes.

SOCIAL/EMOTIONAL DEVELOPMENT

By observation, James appears to relate more successfully with adults than he does, by report, with children his age. This may be a function of the tolerance that adults can demonstrate. For example, James' repetitive talk of lawn mowers, tractors, and cutting grass would soon prove to be annoying and noxious to other children. In addition, apparently he is unaware of social cues, both verbal and nonverbal, that other children may be using to indicate their disinterest in what he is talking about... James is unaware of his impact on others and is unable to read particularly non-verbal and gestural social information from other children. Moreover, he appears to lack basic skills in listening and attending to others by which to better understand these social messages.

CONCLUSIONS/RECOMMENDATIONS

There is a substantial and highly significant difference between James' verbal and non-verbal abilities in favor of the former. In addition, James is exhibiting inattentive behaviors which can adversely affect his performance on school tasks and a significant weakness in his ability to process social information. James, then, is presenting with a number of characteristics that, when considered together, suggest Nonverbal Learning Disability... James will require careful monitoring in the succeeding years to assess the degree to which NLD interferes with his functioning as well as to the development of any further attentional difficulties.

Both reports concluded that ongoing occupational therapy would be critical for Jimmy, and that there should be consistent consultation with his classroom teacher to ensure that his curriculum incorporate several accommodations/modifications, including the following:

- predictable and consistent routine
- use of a picture/schedule board to help Jimmy understand his environment and what is expected of him
- provision of additional time for transition from one activity to the next
- provision of verbal cues to negotiate transitions and to prepare Jimmy in advance for any changes in daily routine (i.e. field trips, vacation days, etc.)
- figures of speech, idioms, or sarcasm should *not* be used; all speech should be specific and literal
- Jimmy should be allowed to verbalize and have verbal feedback in learning situations.
- written tasks may be problematic and Jimmy should be provided with alternative means of demonstrating his knowledge.

The need for social skills training was emphasized as well, to improve eye contact, turn taking, and the ability to deal with novel social situations. We were referred to books and articles by Sue Thompson, MA, CET, as well as by Byron Rourke, PhD, two notable experts in the field.

After reading the report, we felt like we had walked into the middle of a movie; not a movie we necessarily planned to see, either. We didn't know how it started. We were confused about what was happening at the point where we entered, and we sure as heck had no idea how it was going to end. But we couldn't leave, so we just settled in for the long haul.

Dealing with the diagnosis: A to-do list

My grandmother used to say, "Be careful what you wish for, because you just might get it." This describes some of what Dave and I felt as we began processing the information that we received from the folks at CCMC. We wanted to know what was wrong, what was making Jimmy struggle so in his world, yet, now that we had a so-called explanation, being a bit in the dark didn't seem like such an awful alternative. I remember sitting at the kitchen table, reading the report over and over again, hoping that the whole nebulous concept of nonverbal learning disability would somehow become clear, like a blurry image in a pair of binoculars that transforms after a few simple twists of the lenses. There was so much about it that I didn't understand, and I was frustrated by the fact that there wasn't a simpler explanation.

We went into "information-gathering mode" and researched everything available in order to gain an exact understanding of what Jimmy was facing. But going overboard at this juncture leaves you, well, drowning in information, thirsting for knowledge. Some of the information is good, but some is not applicable to you and, in the worst case, downright incorrect. It is very important to take a measured approach to such research. In other words, don't do what we did and park yourself in front of the computer reading every single word available on NLD from clinical reports to chat rooms to dramatic, extremist tales of what could happen down the road. After a few hours of this I was not only exhausted, but quite certain that Jimmy would never enjoy another happy day in his life, ever.

A more tempered and less emotional approach to gathering information ultimately proved the most helpful. During the first few months after receiving the diagnosis, we found the following steps to be the most productive:

1. Start a notebook.

2. Understand your role.

3. Learn how to deal productively with people.

4. Talk to the school.

5. Join a parental support group or other organization.

6. SEPTA.

7. Read, read, read.

8. Search the internet.

9. Sit back, relax and enjoy the show.

Start a notebook

I cannot emphasize enough the importance of this one, simple act which will become the cornerstone in advocating for your NLD child. Buy a large, three-ring binder and place in it every piece of correspondence, every report, every note you take from meetings with doctors, therapists, teachers, etc., and *keep the binder current*. You will be surprised at how quickly you will amass information and, more importantly, how useful it will be to always have a central reference location when you need to pinpoint a detail or recall a conversation that you had (that you were certain you would never forget but of course did). It is difficult enough to keep track of all the details of daily life. When you have a child who requires assistance from any number of professionals in a given year, proper record keeping is essential, not only to track your child's progress and understand his needs, but also to be able to speak to issues which will certainly arise throughout his educational life. Furthermore, this notebook can prove to be the evidence which convinces a program director to fork over services if push comes to shove. Remember: no one can be held accountable for conversations or meetings with persons whose names and titles you do not remember, on dates you cannot recall, about topics which you cannot clearly discuss (CACLD 1999, mailing to members: "Suggestions for Parents").

I am now on my third binder for Jimmy, and have included in these binders everything from correspondence with professionals to homework samples. I sometimes sit and just glance back through the binders to remind myself of the journey my son has taken so far. You would be surprised at all the details you can forget in a short period of time. The binder serves as a reminder of the struggles, the victories, the work and the progress. And it can make you feel very proud indeed, just to flip through it.

Understand your role

No one knows your child like you do. You will be the primary coordinator and decision maker throughout his young life, and it is your *right* to understand the diagnosis and the reasons behind all of the treatment recommendations and educational placements. Nothing should happen without your prior knowledge, understanding and consent. It's that simple. You are not simply an innocent bystander in this process. I become easily frustrated by parents who present themselves in this manner. Since you are, after all, ultimately responsible for your child's care and development, it is of the utmost importance that you take charge in this vital role that you are now playing to bolster his physical, emotional, and educational future. It's important for the obvious reason, of course, that you are his best and most effective advocate, yes. But it is also essential for you and for him so that each can see the other doing what they do, because these synergies are not only magical but they are powerfully effective as well.

While I believe it is always better to err on the side of grace and humility in most situations that life presents to us, I don't believe that parents of special needs children should feel that they are imposing on school systems by requesting services for their children. I say this only because I have heard these sentiments spoken at various meetings, and I feel that it is a disservice to those children. All of our children, regardless of their learning styles or learning needs, are entitled to be taught in the way that they need to be taught so that they can learn. This is a concept that should be unilaterally applied, and if it means that some students require additional services to make it happen, then so be it. In our public school system we choose to call that "special education"—fine. Whatever it takes to get the job done, then we do it. But we're not asking for something "over the top"—we're just asking for whatever it takes to teach our children the way they need to learn.

Learn how to deal productively with people

Being successful as an advocate for your child will depend heavily on your ability to work with the people who work with your child. You should understand up front that you may find some resistance to the idea of becoming included in the required decision-making processes. The most important aspect of this, however, is how you handle this resistance. In this regard, there are two phrases that come to mind:

The squeaky wheel gets the grease.

You catch more flies with honey than with vinegar.

Granted, some situations call for one, some for the other, others for a bit of both. Although some situations will definitely require that you "piss in the soup" (one of my dear Dad's favorite expressions) to get things going, on the whole, when it comes to dealing with the various personalities and situations involved in advocating for your NLD child, honey gets you a lot further than squeaking. In other words, much of your job will be to exercise your diplomatic muscle and maintain a level head. Although it might look great on the silver screen, pounding fists and slamming doors really do not move a meeting along very well at all. Keeping cool and confident and knowing your stuff, these are the ingredients for a tête-à-tête that will get you both noticed and heard. You are a vital member of the team, and you are there to help your child. Grandstanding might feel good for a moment, but it really won't help matters in the long run.

Talk to the school

Ideally, if your child is attending school, the school staff were instrumental in obtaining the NLD diagnosis. However, if your child was left "undiscovered" in the school setting, you must communicate the diagnosis to the school immediately and call for a meeting (referred to in the US as a Planning and Placement Team meeting, or PPT) with the child's teacher and the special education staff to develop an Individualized Educational Program (IEP) for your child. If you contact the school by phone, follow up the call with a letter. Make a note of the contact and, of course, keep this and a copy of the letter in your notebook. I will discuss more about dealing with the school in Chapter 9.

Join a parental support group or other organization

By talking with others who share your situation, you can gain perspective, moral support, and avoid feeling alone. Get information about different services that are available, and other parents' opinions about these services. Join any local organizations that are active in the learning disability community (LD) so that you can get on mailing lists for local conferences, lectures and workshops (see Resources list at the end of the book). Many schools have support groups for parents of special needs children, which is a good way to share concerns and information and to identify other children in the school (not necessarily in your child's class) who might be good candidates for play dates and other activities.

If you can't find a support group for parents of special needs children in your community, then consider starting one. Chances are that there are plenty of parents who would love to share their thoughts and feelings with other parents, but are feeling too awkward or unsure to speak up. The school won't be able to give you any information whatsoever on other special needs families because of confidentiality laws. However, you can certainly send a general flyer out to the entire school inviting any parents of special needs children to attend a support group meeting, and then hope that some will attend and sign up for future meetings.

Special Education Parent Teacher Association (SEPTA)

Many school districts also have a Special Education Parent Teacher Association (SEPTA) which is part of the regular PTA group. When I moved to Redding, Connecticut, three years ago, there was neither an active SEPTA nor support group for parents of special needs children. I attended a SEPTA informational meeting and helped out on some organizational and planning ideas. I am now president, and we have a membership of nearly 30 families. A lot can change in a year! This will be discussed in further detail later in the book (see Chapter 14).

Read, read, read

There are numerous books on NLD available in bookstores as well as by catalog and on the internet. Several that come to mind are:

- *Nonverbal Learning Disabilities at Home: A Parent's Guide* (Tanguay 2001)

- *The Source for Nonverbal Learning Disorders* (Thompson 1997)

- *Helping a Child with Nonverbal Learning Disorder or Asperger's Syndrome* (Stewart 2002)

- *Teaching Your Child the Language of Social Success* (Duke, Nowicki and Martin 1996)

- *Bridging the Gap: Raising a Child with Nonverbal Learning Disorder* (Whitney 2002).

I have listed the details of all recommended reading in the Bibliography at the end of the book.

Search the internet

When used properly, the internet is a valuable research tool, so by all means use it. I have found many great resources there, from articles to websites and Q&A forums (also in the Resources list). As with everything else, however, you must exercise care and moderation. Like chocolate, a little is very good, but more is not necessarily better (even though it may seem to be at first).

Sit back, relax and enjoy the show

Through the frenetic search for answers, information, interventions, specialists, support groups, articles and the like, the parents of an NLD child risk becoming robotically driven to find answers, and burned out by their relentless desire to help. As my husband, an accomplished runner, so eloquently pointed out to me on one particularly driven type of day, "Remember honey, this is not a sprint, it's a marathon." Make sure to reserve time in the day to simply enjoy your family and to allow them to enjoy you—the parent, not the advocate. Sit on the couch and chat, take a special trip to the library or the movies. Give each other down time, and don't try to make every waking minute a teaching one. Above all, let your NLD child be who he is, and let yourself be who you are, because those times are precious and the memories of them are pure magic.

When the blur finally subsided and Dave and I were able to condense the information we gathered, we found ourselves relieved that, finally, we had something to grasp, some way to begin to understand the differences that our son had to live with; differences which, up to that moment, had probably made him feel like a stranger in his own skin. Armed with these tools of information and intervention we, as parents, became committed to understanding our son's world and to helping him learn how best to navigate the chaos that surrounded him.

The pool party

On a warm summer day when my son Jimmy was five years old, I took him to a friend's sixth birthday party which was to take place in his backyard pool.

When we had first arrived at the party, Jimmy was excited to see his friend, to go swimming in the pool, to have cake and ice cream. The rest of the commotion that awaited him, however, was nothing short of a nightmare. Jimmy cautiously approached the group of nearly 25 children playing with pool toys and spraying each other with water guns. The fact that the atmosphere was jovial was completely lost on him, who could process nothing but the new and quite threatening nature of the scene. I tried to lure him to a quiet corner of the pool where we could play together and kill time or, better still, wait until one of the other children showed some interest in him.

At home later on, Jimmy asked me, "Mommy, why am I so wrong?" I told him, as lovingly as I could, that there was nothing whatsoever "wrong" with him, and that sometimes a party or an outing just doesn't "click," for whatever reason. I added that I wasn't much for parties when I was a kid either and I still wasn't (which wasn't a lie). Then I watched my boy go to sleep.

It was much more difficult than it had been when he was younger and I brought him to toddler parties where parallel play was par for the course. He was always quite happy to play with me in those circumstances—at least until cake and ice cream were served—and then he would take his goodie bag and toddle off to home, grubby, full and happy. The difference here was that Jimmy was well aware of his being outside of the group, and this was upsetting to him. Although my presence was necessary to maintain a certain comfort level for him, I was no longer sufficient.

When the kids were all called out of the pool for organized games, I could tell that Jimmy was struggling with the idea of trying to join in, but he just couldn't get himself to do it. I also struggled with whether or not I should push him, frustrated with his indecision and his unwillingness to try. The pool was now quiet and empty — he could have it all to himself, but that wasn't what he wanted at all. I sat at the edge, a fake smile spread across my face as if my swimsuit was too tight, now trying to encourage Jimmy to swim with me. Instead, he sidled up next to me, laid his head on my lap and began to cry. "I want to go home," he said. So we did.

Summary

1. After his NLD diagnosis, initial modifications for Jimmy included: predictable and consistent routine; use of visual aids in the classroom; additional time and verbal cues to assist in transitions; no use of sarcasm in speech.

2. Things to do when you find out your child has NLD include: Keep a notebook for all correspondence; understand your role as advocate for your child; learn how to deal productively with the team; talk to the school regularly; join a parental support group or other organization; become involved in a Special Education PTA (SEPTA); and read and research information about NLD.

3. You are your child's primary advocate and it is your right to understand the reason behind all treatment recommendations and educational placements.

4. Being a successful advocate for your NLD child depends on your ability to work effectively and diplomatically with his educational team. This includes your ability to effectively handle resistance, should it arise.

5. Be sure to reserve time to enjoy your child and just be parents.

Chapter 3

At Home

Parenting the NLD Child

My religion is kindness.

The Dalai Lama

Picture this: you arrive home from the hospital with a bundle full of baby and a feeling of complete and utter helplessness. You sit, gingerly at best, next to your husband on the couch and stare at your new infant, wrinkled and asleep in his infant carrier. The silence of the child is unnerving, like the calm before a hurricane, and you both wish you had some faint idea of what to do next.

These were the feelings that I recall when receiving Jimmy's diagnosis of NLD in 1999. The report arrived right after our family had returned home from a two-week beach vacation. My brain and body somewhat shriveled from sun and sea, I read the evaluation half expecting to see that it had all been a great misunderstanding; that my son was merely a keenly intelligent child with eccentricities who needed to be put in a highly challenging academic environment fast. Instead, I was confronted with the nebulous term nonverbal learning disability and found myself wishing that the report came with some sort of manual to walk me through this confusing disorder, this vast new world that our family had been thrust into. However, as is the case with most of life's little surprises, we had to start from scratch.

As a matter of fact, starting from scratch was not restricted to our search for information about Jimmy's disability. As far as our methods of parenting were concerned we had to pretty much do the same thing. Dave and I soon learned that most of the "traditional" methods of discipline we had been exposed to as children and had assumed we would employ as parents were not going to work well with Jimmy. We had to learn to think and communicate with our child in a totally new and different way.

There is a very vivid memory in my mind of the first time I took my baby Jimmy out in public. Dave and I went to dinner at a TGI Friday's in Waterbury, Connecticut. I brought Jimmy into the restaurant in his car seat, which I carefully placed on the bench seat of the booth where we were seated. If you've ever been in one of those restaurants, you've seen all the memorabilia they have hanging from the ceilings and the walls. They're usually fun, noisy places to eat, but the evening I brought my baby there, it was a different experience.

It was then that I realized the ferocity that was motherhood, the strength and adrenaline attached to the protective instinct. I couldn't possibly relax. I suddenly grew several pairs of eyes, fangs and claws, and there was nothing that could come near my baby. Yes, I was teetering on insanity from lack of sleep and two cracked and bleeding nipples from breastfeeding, but I had to resist the urge to arch my arms over the child every time a waiter so much as walked by. It was a feeling I had never experienced before, and it was neither pleasant nor controllable. It was nature taking over.

While we learn to temper these instincts somewhat with the passage of time, they never go away, even when our children learn to tie their shoes, ride a bike, drive a car, pay a mortgage. But we, as parents, must increasingly veil our attempts to protect our children, lest we teach them overdependence and the whole growing up thing completely backfires. Because of the challenges that many NLD children face, it may prove exceedingly difficult for the parent to take the needed step back. You won't at first, because you won't be able to. If, as was the case with Jimmy, the NLD child is your firstborn, you'll be hard pressed to ever let up, but eventually you'll see that taking a step back is the only way to teach your child to stand up for himself. If you give him the tools he needs, you'll share the satisfaction he feels at using them.

Discipline

"Talking back"

Growing up in my parents' house, the thought of questioning one of my parents' instructions in any way, shape or form was considered "talking back"—behavior as unacceptable as standing on the dinner table and hurling mashed potatoes at my sister. It was a no-no that was ingrained in us at an early age and went unquestioned, like curse words, cutting class, or neglecting to do our homework. But this is precisely the kind of no-no that, as a parent of an NLD child, you simply must let go of. At first glance, it seems unconscionable—"I'm going to let my child question my directions, my authority? There will be total chaos in the house, not to mention the fact that I will lose credibility with the other children." Yes, those thoughts did cross my mind but, if you approach this kind of parenting in a logical way, and consider the way your NLD child is approaching his end of the process, you will be able to make it work.

For example, whenever we instruct Jimmy not to do something, he almost always asks why. At first, our knee-jerk reaction as parents (borne of our own upbringing) was to reprimand him for questioning our authority, but we soon realized that his question was rooted not in defiance but in true curiosity. He did not understand, for example, why we didn't want him to do what he was doing, and he asked because he wanted to know. It really was that simple. Whereas a neurologically typical (NT) child might follow the direction while silently summing up the situation at hand, there is no silent summing up of the situation for the NLD child. This is a fundamental fact that, as parents, we must accept and therefore should not be surprised when there are questions resulting from our requests of our children. Our son needed to know what he did that wasn't acceptable. If he didn't ask, then he wouldn't learn and very well might do the same thing again, be reprimanded again, ask why again, and the cycle would continue.

So, as parents, we had to train ourselves to break everything down to its literal parts, because that's how our son interpreted his world. Once we understood this and got into the habit of explaining ourselves and our directions a bit more clearly and specifically, we found that Jimmy would follow them quite happily and the stress would be removed from the situation. On the other hand, if we withheld explanation and forced him to obey without it, his level of stress and anxiety would escalate, not because of defiance, but because of confusion and frustration.

It is essential to note here that consistency must be maintained. If one parent accepts the child's questioning and explains the reasoning behind their instructions patiently, while the other parent becomes agitated and responds with an annoyed tone, the result will be confusion to the NLD child as well as to any siblings in the household. As with any parenting methods, a unified approach is very important. But in this case, it may be even more important that both parents follow similar language patterns since the NLD child is so keenly tapped into the verbal aspects of his world.

Reprimand

When things get a little out of control and we parents feel that the NLD child needs to be reprimanded in some way, it is important that we keep in mind all of the concepts that we have already discussed here. That is, just because we are trying to instill a lesson regarding something that we feel was done in error, that doesn't mean we want to send a message that the child is "bad" or "shameful", thus possibly leading to a depressive state or to a point where the child's self-esteem is harmed. For example, the often used method of "time outs" in a closed room is not recommended for the NLD child. On the other hand, if the NLD child is acting out in a violent manner, I would not hesitate to say to him, "It seems to me that you need to have some quiet time, and I want to give you what you need, so why don't you go up to your room for a while by yourself?' If, at that point, he resists the idea vehemently, then I will remind him that he must stop the behavior immediately or I will suggest again that he'll have to go to his room. If he continues the behavior, I must make good on my promise, or I will lose credibility with him, leading to more frustration. NLD children are children, after all, and they derive comfort from knowing their boundaries.

Of course, these scenarios don't always play out in the manner I've written them here. I would sincerely love to say, even fantasize that they have, but the fact is that all parents are human. I have made some horrible mistakes with my son. I have raised my voice to him out of sheer frustration. I've even locked myself in the bathroom a few times. Each time I've done these things, I've apologized to him, and learned that all that he heard was a high pitched noise and all he saw was a very upset mom. There was no useful communication passing between us at all. If anything, I would hope that you will all learn from my mistakes.

When your NLD child exhibits unacceptable behavior, there is no better resolution than to speak to him in a calm voice about the reason that you didn't like the behavior and how it should have been done differently. Eye contact, firmness of voice, repetition if necessary, these will get the point across. If you feel that there should be repercussions for the action, then perhaps that should be discussed. My husband and I have found that any kind of withholding of privileges having to do with a current perseveration (fixation) is pretty much off limits. For example, if Jimmy is locked onto a certain computer game at the moment, we would never use that as a "teaching" tool and take away his privileges as a disciplinary measure because it would only raise his anxiety level to such a fever pitch that the child wouldn't learn anything from the process at all. The point here is: *use your head.* You know what the hot buttons are, so don't push them. Discipline is intended to teach, not throw wood on a fire.

The "meltdown"

In our house, we refer to a severe bout of anxiety as a "meltdown" because, well, that's exactly what happens. Our son might begin to sob uncontrollably and even fall to the floor. Make no mistake about it, when these things happen it upsets everyone in the house. At these times it is essential for a parent to keep his cool and to provide, through body language, tone of voice, facial expressions and every other possible way, the comfort the child is obviously desperate for. This may be in the form of a hug, a tender word or just quiet accompaniment. Raising your voice is simply out of the question—there's no other way to put it. This goes for your communication with your child, your spouse, other siblings, everyone in the vicinity. Not only because it causes anxiety, but also it's completely counterproductive. *It adds stress to an already stressful situation.* Besides that, the NLD child won't hear a thing you're saying. He'll only hear the noise and the volume and it will do nothing but dig the hole he's already in deeper, so don't do it. Control yourself. Leave the room if you have to and gather your composure. The most important thing to remember is that piling on to the situation will only make matters worse. We've all felt overloaded at times. NLD children feel overloaded more often than not, so take two seconds to think about that and you may be able to hold your tongue. Remember: try to look at things the way they are seeing them, and it may be a little easier to hold it together.

The "put-down"

There isn't any constructive reason to put another person down, whether it be a child, adult, co-worker, neighbor, sibling, friend, retailer or telemarketer. Put-downs are particularly insidious when dealing with the NLD child, who is often struggling with low self-esteem to begin with. A generally good rule of thumb is as follows: turn your words to the positive and never say anything that could be interpreted as a put-down to your child, ever. There isn't a single reason to do it, and it won't serve any purpose but to make him feel bad about himself, which in turn reduces his ability to function. This has been found to be true over and over again.

I know that this should go without saying, but a corollary to the "no put-down" rule is the "no name calling" rule. When I say this among a group of parents, you would be surprised how many of them roll their eyes as if to say "Well, of course not!" However, we often practice name calling without realizing it, and it can be extremely damaging to the self-esteem of any child, the NLD child certainly being no exception. If you've ever said to your son or daughter "Are you going to clear the table tonight, or are you going to be a lazybones?" then I'm afraid you're guilty of name calling. Or how about a time when he ran to tell you about a rule that his brother or sister broke and you might have said to him, "Nobody likes a tattletale."Once again, this would qualify as name calling, even though you might be trying to teach him a valuable life lesson.

While, understandably, these examples are certainly not intended to hurt our children's feelings in any way, the point here is that there really isn't any great purpose behind these names and, therefore, any need in using them. We can accomplish the same goals by talking through these lessons with the NLD child and ditching the name calling which, to the NLD brain, is on par with sarcasm and colloquialisms—they really don't "compute." The bottom line is, stick to clear, plain language and talk things through with your child.

Self-esteem

A valuable benchmark to use in all matters of parenting an NLD child is "In what way will this affect his self-esteem?" This applies to everything from play dates to birthday parties to chores around the house and, like most everything else we talk about in this book (and for most parenting issues across the board, for that matter), *consistency is key.*

Household chores are a perfect example of this. By assigning chores to your child you are giving him the opportunity to take responsibility for some of the workload around the house and to pitch in. In so doing, he feels important and grown up and, if you play your cards right, everyone can even have a little fun in the process. It is essential, however, when assigning chores to your NLD child, to keep in mind a few key thoughts:

1. *Be specific.* Your child is going to listen to your instructions quite literally, so make sure you are explaining the job just the way you want it done but with short, easy to understand directions. Don't give him three or four tasks in a row. One thing to do at a time is all he can handle, or he'll forget the next thing and become quite frustrated and anxious. You can also write a list for an older child, or have him write it.

2. *Positive reinforcement.* Remember to give positive comments first ("great try"), even if the job isn't done to your liking. You can show ways to improve in a gentle and supportive way without deflating your child's self-esteem.

3. *Be accessible.* Answer the questions which will surely arise.

While your child will certainly help lighten your workload, keep in mind that the positive feedback he receives from you and the resulting boost to his self-esteem will go much further in the long run. This doesn't mean to tell him the job is perfect when it isn't, this means to tell him that he did the best he could do which was what you were after in the first place. Smudges on mirrors can be removed, but those on a child's self-worth are much less soluble.

Training yourself to speak in NLD language

Once you've learned how your NLD child views his world—which is an accomplishment in itself—it is essential that you modify your language to accommodate such a view. That is, you must speak to your child in a way that is easily understood by him. The NLD child is both a literal thinker and speaker. Colloquialisms, vernacular, and sarcasm are not only ineffective with these children, but they can also cause misunderstanding and anxiety for them. Similarly, you must always keep in mind the intentions behind what your child is saying. By this I mean that literal thought can translate into what sounds like blunt, even rude statements. This is not the aim of the NLD child. Like most children, they are motivated to please, to fit in. Still, their view of the world is black and white, and they can only sort through it using verbal expression. Add to the mix a tendency for literal language and you've got a kid that calls 'em as he sees 'em. That can be a bit off-putting. For example, consider this exchange between an NLD child and his parent over the dinner table:

Parent: Would you like a piece of steak?

Child: There is blood on the plate.

Parent: That's the juice from the steak.

Child: It's gross.

Parent: It's better not to call it blood. We call it juice.

Child: But it's really blood, isn't it?

Parent: Yes, but please don't talk about that at the dinner table. I'll cut up some for you.

Child: I don't want any steak because the juice is gross.

Parent: Then just say no thank you.

Child: No thank you.

If something like this occurs, and language comes out sounding harsh, try not to react in a negative way. If we do (and, yes, sometimes we do) we find that it frustrates Jimmy to the point of tears, often because he feels we don't believe him when he says he didn't mean to offend us. We try to explain to him how we feel he could have expressed himself better, keeping the language as straightforward as possible but with a smooth edge. This is always a tricky situation because we know that, in polite conversation, there is no way that certain types of comments won't be interpreted as rude, no matter what our son's intentions are. We tell him that although we believe that he didn't mean any offense, others might not understand. It's that simple, and no amount of explaining will change it. So we try to impress upon our son how simple changes in wording can make a big difference in the way people respond to you and to the way you speak to them. In the above example, we would explain to Jimmy that the best way to handle the "steak" situation would be to simply say "No, thank you" to the offer of steak and to withhold any further comment on the meat's appearance, etc. because it might offend the other people dining at the table.

Take note: you cannot assume that such lessons in conversational skills will be readily applied in other situations. The NLD child has trouble applying what he learns from one situation to another in all cases, so gentle reminders in a safe, low-stress environment (like home) of appropriate conversational practices can serve as positive reinforcement.

The 67 Ps: Patience, patience, patience, patience…you get the idea

All I can say about this particular topic is that, if you think you are a patient person to begin with and can therefore gloss over this section, get down off your high horse and think again. When you're the parent of an NLD child, patience isn't just a virtue, it's a necessity. You will be required to exercise this one to the very best of your ability, not just when you're well rested and fresh as a daisy. These children, while they bring endless joy and richness to our lives, have the ability to frazzle our nerves like no one else can. Why? Because when we become parents we don't hand in our membership cards to the human club. As humans, it is perfectly normal to get just a little annoyed when your kid talks to you nonstop or carries on loquacious monologues about hairdryers or lawn mowers or whatever it is that they're fixating on at the moment. And that's on a good day, when you're not already reaching your limit because of something that's happening at work, or because of an argument you're having with a friend or husband or sister or another child or because you're coming down with a cold. So, when you think you're about to implode, like you cannot possibly hear another utterance out of their mouths, you must dig very deep down, and I mean very deep down to those parts unknown where only parents can go and find that secret chamber of patience (very Harry Potteresque, don't you think?) to draw from. When this happens to me, which it certainly does, I am reminded of a very sage piece of advice I received from Dr. Byron Rourke when we brought Jimmy to his office in Canada to be evaluated in 2001. He said that when things get difficult for us, we must try to imagine how the world must seem to Jimmy. That was like a cold bucket of water on Dave and me, one which we continue to throw on each other, without hesitation, whenever necessary.

No switcharoonies

We've talked about the need for sticking to routines and plans, and I know this is not always possible. But, for the NLD child, I cannot emphasize enough how disruptive it can be to do a switcharoonie: for example, to tell your child that after school you're going to go to the grocery store and then to the library, but after he gets off the bus to tell him that you've changed your mind and decided to go to the library the next day and wait until dad gets home to do the grocery shopping. It may seem like a little thing to us, but nothing is a little thing to the NLD child. Once he sets a certain plan in his mind, it is extremely difficult for him to change on a dime and readjust to a new one, no matter what the nature of the plan was. When you consider the backlash that you're going to have to deal with when you spring that last minute change on him, you just might want to consider sticking to the original plan—and next time keeping your mouth shut until you're dead sure you're going to do what you say you're going to do.

There's another mouse in the house—the sibling dynamic

Our daughter Shawn is almost two years younger than Jimmy and has always been adoring of her brother. They are very different in personality and comport, but are extremely tolerant and accepting of each other. We have never formally discussed Jimmy's differences with Shawn, as we believe she is too young to participate in such a discussion, but we will explain individual "episodes" if we believe an explanation is warranted. For instance, when Jimmy melted down after several classmates didn't answer the phone when he called to invite them over, I noticed that Shawn was hiding behind the kitchen door looking very agitated. Once Jimmy left the room, I coaxed her out from behind the door and discussed the situation with her:

Mom: Are you upset because Jimmy is upset?

[Shawn nodded.]

Mom: He's upset because his friends didn't answer the phone.

Shawn: Why didn't he just leave a message?

Mom: He thinks they won't call him back.

Shawn: They won't call him back if he doesn't leave a message.

Mom: He thinks they won't anyway.

Shawn: Of course they will! Why does Jimmy get so cranky about this stuff?

Mom: Because he thinks the kids don't like him.

Shawn: They like him.

Mom: I know. But he doesn't think so. He's just feeling that way right now.

Shawn: Well he shouldn't.

Mom: But telling him that won't make him feel better. So let's just show him we love him in our own way, okay?

[Shawn nodded again.]

In a family where one child has special needs and the other child is neurologically typical (NT), it may happen that the special needs child requires quite a bit of attention, whether it be emotional or physical, daily or on a cumulative basis over a week or month's period. It is therefore important to make sure that the NT child is given adequate "alone" time with each parent so that he/she does not feel slighted in any way. This can be accomplished in a variety of ways, by choosing some extracurricular activities that one or the other parent can take the child to, such as music, dance or athletic activities, or simply by allocating a day during the week to spend alone with that child. Even bath time can be a special time between one parent and child. Shawn is very interested in ballet and piano, and these are special activities that she does and that I take a special interest in with her. We work our schedules around so that she can take these each week, and Jimmy often accompanies us when we take her to and from the lessons. She feels special and lucky to take them, and really enjoys her time there. Our piano practice time during the week serves as special alone time for Shawn and me.

Another very important point here: all of the suggestions and tactics mentioned can also serve as models to teach siblings how to deal with the NLD member of the family and, incidentally, are not bad life and social skills lessons in general. Throughout the various situations that we as parents face with our NLD children, it is important to reinforce with their sibling(s) why we are making these accommodations and why it is important that we remain consistent with our approach both in the home and away from home. We must impress upon the sibling(s) that, when they are away from home with their NLD brother or sister, they play an important role as advocate for that sibling.

Let me stop here for a moment. Don't get me wrong. I live in the real world and am fully aware that there are limits to what a sibling will do in the school environment on behalf of a brother or sister. But by being made aware of these issues, the sibling can at least perhaps diffuse a potentially bad situation for her NLD brother/sister.

Parents: On being a couple

It's important for any couple with children to find time alone together, to enjoy some uninterrupted time enjoying each other's company. For those with an NLD child, it is particularly important. The structured environment that one must create for the child can make spontaneity seem like a distant memory. You become extremely good at the parenting partnership, a well-oiled machine in fact, and you may very well forget what it's like to go out to a movie, a dinner or a weekend away and have a conversation about something, anything besides the latest PPT, IEP, the amazing social strides he's made, that thing he did yesterday, the latest fixation, and on and on. I'm not saying there's any shame in that, because it's a trap we can all fall into, and Dave and I have. But it's important that you recognize when this is happening, and take steps to control it so that you don't lose sight of that fact that you're still a couple and you still have a relationship outside of the parenting partnership. After all, that's what started the whole ball rolling to begin with, right?

The point is that, in order to be the best parents you can be, you need to rejuvenate the relationship that got you there in the first place. The tendency is to feel pangs of guilt if you take your attention away from the needs of the children for a second, primarily because their needs, particularly those of the NLD child, are so high so much of the time. But what ends up happening after a while is that the well gets tapped dry and you suffer from burnout. When this happens, you're no good to anyone at all. By returning to your relationship as a couple you replenish the well a bit and you can provide the energy and enthusiasm that you need back to the parenting part of your life. Believe me, it will all be there waiting for you after dinner and a movie, and everyone will survive quite nicely.

Summary

1.   Because of the differences in the way NLD children process information, traditional parenting techniques often don't work with them. Parents should learn how to speak more directly and with more explanation when administering discipline, reprimands and consequences. The NLD child often asks for the rationale behind these for understanding and clarification, not to be defiant or impudent.

2.   Severe bouts of anxiety, or meltdowns, may happen frequently. It is important for other family members to stay calm and even-tempered to help the child regain composure.

3.   The NLD child can sometimes experience low self-esteem. Some strategies to enhance self-esteem include refraining from put-downs, inclusion in household chores, and avoidance of colloquialisms, vernacular and sarcasm when speaking to the child.

4.   It is essential that parents modify their language to accommodate how the NLD child views his world—as a literal thinker and speaker.

5.   For parents of NLD children, patience is not just a virtue, it's a necessity.

6.   Avoid changes of plans or schedule ("switcharoonies") wherever possible.

7. In a family where one child has special needs and another child is neurologically typical (NT), it is important to make sure that the NT child is given adequate "alone" time with each parent.

8. It is important for parents to set aside time to be a couple.

Chapter 4

Managing Inflow
The Kid in the Candy Store

**One doesn't discover new lands without consenting to
lose sight of the shore for a very long time.**

André Gide

I remember as a young girl being taken by my uncle to the
neighborhood penny candy store on Sunday afternoons and standing
in front of huge glass counters which housed enormous choices of
candies of all sorts. Wax bottles full of sweet syrups, red chewy pennies
that stuck in my teeth, the ubiquitous fireball, caramels, jujubes, licorice
shoe strings, you name it—they were all there for the asking. All I had to
do was choose, and it was a wonderful decision to have to make. I was,
quite literally, the "kid in the candy store."

For the NLD child, however, being the kid in the candy store can be
an extremely unpleasant and overwhelming experience leading to debilitating anxiety. These children don't function well in a situation where
they are bombarded by stimuli and faced with numerous choices. They
are better able to process information when it is delivered to them in a
calm, sequential and controlled manner.

Imagine a neurologically typical (NT) child walking into a video
store with the objective of renting a video to watch during the evening.
Maybe she has something in mind: an animated feature or a live action
thriller. So, she goes in and makes her way to the family movie section,
perusing a couple of the new releases along the way and maybe even
getting sidetracked by one or two in the process. The NLD child, on the
other hand, has an entirely different experience. He walks into the store
and immediately finds himself confronted by a wall of color and sound

as people mill around shelves upon shelves of video boxes. The excessive amount of visual stimuli makes it very difficult for the child to approach his task calmly, and he becomes easily agitated. This is complicated by the fact that people are continually walking in front of him (additional visual stimulation and distraction) and possibly even bumping into him (tactile stimulation and distraction). There is music and chatter in the background, and his parents are probably asking him if he'd like this or that movie.

Dave came up with the phrase "managing inflow" while we were chatting with the school psychologist one day about trying to minimize the static in our son's life, and it seemed to capture the idea so well that it stuck. As parents, we have to understand that the manner in which the NLD brain processes information makes the excessive "inflow" of stimuli an unpleasant experience for our child. Therefore, it is our job to attempt to "manage the inflow" so that our child can go at a pace that is more comfortable for him. This might mean verbally offering a set of choices before even entering the video store so that our child doesn't have to mentally subject himself to the entire selection. These excessive stimuli can come in many forms. Let's review some of the most frequently occurring ones.

Parties

When it comes to parties, I'm probably not the right one to ask because I've never really liked them. Maybe there's a neurological reason for it or maybe I've just been to a lot of bad parties. All that being said, when it comes to parties and the NLD child, as parents we must make sure to always have a plan in place so that if the child becomes overwhelmed or uncomfortable, we can simply remove him from the situation or at least give him some kind of safe haven to escape to.

In a vacuum, I would simply say that there is no situation which warrants staying at a party if your NLD child is freaking out or over-whelmed by the crowd, noise or commotion. Just make a swift and graceful exit, and, if the host's or hostess's nose gets out of joint because of your early departure, tough darts. However, I also understand that in the real world we can't run over the top of people and expect our lives to necessarily run smoothly as a result. So, if there is a social event you feel is important that you attend as a family, you might want to talk to the host and/or hostess beforehand, explain the parameters within which you are operating, and look for some guidance from them. They may have an upstairs room where you can duck out for a half hour or so if things get too crazy, or a game room with a videocassette player where you can invite your child to go for a rest and a movie if he gets uncomfortable with the crowd. If the child is too young to be on his own, you can consider bringing a sitter along with you. With a little forward thinking, there are many options that can offer you the opportunity to accept social invitations while still giving your NLD child the security and comfort that he wants and needs.

Hosting a party in the home of an NLD child, even if the child is told about it beforehand, can cause strange behaviors. Let's step back for a moment and take a look from the child's perspective. First of all, a party of grownups represents a mass influx of strangers into the home and is an entirely unnerving experience for the child. It represents novelty of the first order, disruption, noise, chaos, you name it. To top it all off, the guests usually arrive on or about the same time, and there's lots of fanfare about it—high pitched voices, loud greetings, exaggerated facial expressions. If a child is in the area, any guest grownups will go out of their way to give a supercharged greeting to the host's kid, throwing wood on an already raging fire.

A good way to avoid overwhelming the NLD child is to arrange for the guests to arrive on a staggered schedule, with the more familiar guests coming first so that your child can adjust a bit before the rest of the invitees filter in. If it's a surprise party, be sure to talk to the child about that aspect, and offer the option to be out of the room for the big entrance of the honored guest. If it's a child-themed party and any costumed characters are expected, these should be discussed well in advance. The bottom line is, keep the surprise factor to a minimum and, at the very least, offer the NLD child options to bow out. I always give the option of a separate room, a video and a few favorite snack choices set up in advance. If Jimmy wants to be alone for a while, even if there are other children there that want to join him, I allow him the indulgence. It is, after all, his home, his oasis. Usually, he emerges and wants to join the others after a time. But forcing him to be with others would serve no purpose other than to raise stress levels to the point where he would eventually lock himself in his room, and then we're back to square one.

Amusement parks

If you want to talk about stimulus overflow, go no further than the typical school or town carnival, chock full of amusements and thrill. When we plan this type of family outing I know only too well that, after the initial nanoseconds and the excitement fades, the flash flood of stimuli that follows will lead to a meltdown of mammoth proportions. The first hurdle comes with having to choose which ride to take—will it be Jimmy's choice first or his sister's choice? Then, once they actually get on the ride, will they make it to the actual operation of the ride before one or both of them becomes afraid? With all of the noise and commotion, Jimmy may very well become overwhelmed by the whole experience well before the ride begins, and we often find ourselves rushing in to fetch him off the thing before it starts to move. At this point, his little sister wants no part of staying on herself, and the whole thing begins to unravel at a breakneck pace.

Who knows the cause: it may be the multitude of popcorn, cotton candy and caramel apples, the lights on the rides or simply the bumps, knocks and other tactile stimuli that one has to endure while navigating the carnival. Whatever it is, there is simply too much of it, and Jimmy's mind and body simply cannot process it. In these cases, what the parent does not do is most important:

- *Do not show tension on your face or in your actions.* You'll simply fuel an already smoldering fire.

- *Don't interrogate the child as to what's bothering him.* There's too much going on around him, and his brain needs a break. Besides, he doesn't really know what's bothering him, but you should.

- *Take a break.* Try to find a quiet (or quieter) place to sit and calm down the child. Sometimes just watching the rides and the other children will help him acclimate a bit.

- *If there is another sibling, try to allow them to separate a while.* The other one can enjoy the rides by him or herself. If they must be together, have them talk about what they'd like to do next, in what order, etc.

Choices

Sometimes managing inflow can be as simple as just reining in the NLD child's choices. Don't give him an endless array of things to choose from, be it sandwiches for the next day's lunch or shirt colors when you're shopping online. These children become easily overwhelmed, and it's a feeling that unnerves them instantly. You can train yourself to offer two sandwich choices rather than four (offer two today, and the other two tomorrow). There is nothing to be gained from throwing out seven shirt color choices if your child becomes frozen and unable to answer at all: better to narrow it down to three colors and get a quicker response. Parents of NLD children must learn to become master translators and condensers of information until such time as the child himself can learn to take the scads of information out there and weed out what he doesn't want or need. Just take a look at the cereal aisle in the grocery store to know what I'm talking about. When I decide to treat Jimmy by letting him choose a kid's cereal, it's like throwing him into the lion's den. Walking down that aisle is like walking into the fun house at the carnival. There are more names, boxes, colors, and brands than you can shake a stick at. So I simply escort him to that section of the aisle where I know he'll be the most interested and suggest that he choose from three or four of his well-known favorites. Immediately, much of the stress leaves his face and he is able to narrow down to one or two. A few minutes later, we have a winner and we're off to the next item on the grocery list. Mission accomplished, with minimum pain and suffering.

Novelty

I know we've discussed this issue already, but the matter of novelty really can't be mentioned too many times. The introduction of anything new or unexpected to the NLD child is paramount to pulling the proverbial rug out from under him. This doesn't mean that the novel item or event necessarily has to have a negative connotation either. I remember one afternoon when my sister made a surprise visit with her three children to my home. I decided to surprise Jimmy by bringing his cousins in the car with me when I picked him up from school.

Now, let me preface this by saying that Jimmy adores his cousins, but by bringing them in the car with me, I gave him no chance to digest this huge wrench in the works and the resulting change in his daily routine.

While this was undoubtedly a very positive development in his day, it was still a major disruption that he needed to be notified about in advance. When I slid open the door to the van and he saw the three smiling faces sitting inside, he smiled widely because he had been taught that it was the right thing to do, but it was a pained smile, like that of a gassy baby. During the ride home he interrogated me as to why I didn't tell him that they were coming (he simply couldn't accept that I didn't know) and, once we got home, he chose to be alone in his room for a rather extended period of time before he would play with his cousins. Needless to say, his reaction confused his cousins and made the visit awkward at first.

Now, how could I have handled this differently? Surely it isn't always possible to give your NLD child a head's up in the event of an unannounced mid-afternoon visitor, and you're not about to call the school office and have a note passed to your child to alert him. This is not what the school's administrative team is to be used for. However, had I picked Jimmy up at school with only his sister in the car, as usual, and told him on the way home that his cousins were waiting for us at the house, although he might have still taken a while to warm up to the change in routine, he would have at least had that time to digest the information and prepare himself a bit. It might have eliminated some of the awkwardness that we all felt as a result of my poor judgment. The bottom line is: surprise is going to backfire almost every time, so avoid it whenever possible.

Holidays

Major holidays, though wonderful, represent a significant change in routine and a disruption in normalcy. We eat differently, we see people we haven't seen in a long time, we're expected to kiss a lot, smile a lot, act nicer than usual, give gifts, get gifts (and then act as if you like what you get), dress in nice clothes, go visiting, sit for a long time in the car (sometimes while wearing the nice clothes), stay up later than usual, miss favorite television shows, play with cousins, go to church. Must I go on? Talk about excessive inflow—holidays to the NLD child are like an all-you-can-eat buffet when all you really want is tea and toast.

We'll talk more about holidays in Chapter 12, but they are worth mentioning here as they relate to managing inflow. Probably the best way to equip your NLD child for the holidays is to really prepare him.

Try to outline what the schedule will be for visits, meals, outings, religious services, parties, etc., as long in advance as possible with as much detail as possible, and get ready for a lot of questions.

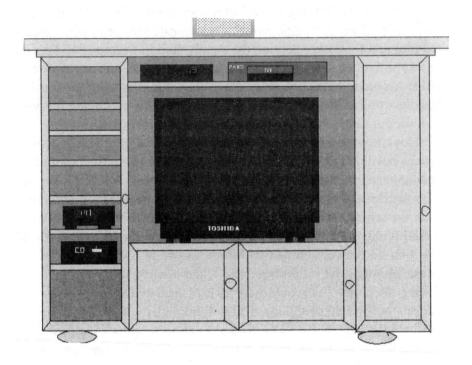

Keep It Simple, Silly (KISS)

Managing inflow, while it sounds like a fancy concept, really isn't. The point is quite the opposite of fancy, in fact. I like to call it Keep It Simple, Silly, or KISS. By this I mean, reduce choices, options and stimuli to the necessary minimum. It will make life a lot more pleasant for your NLD child and, by association, a lot more pleasant for you and your other children.

This reminds me of preparing for my first solo trip to Europe as a college student. I began to pack my suitcase and my father stuck his head around my bedroom door and said, "How's it going?" I said, "Great. I'm almost done." He came back ten minutes later and said, "Done?" I said, "Yep, I think so." He said, "Good. Now take half of it out."

We've discussed parties, visits from relatives, trips to the video store, but the KISS philosophy applies in large part to everyday life, not just to the out of the ordinary events mentioned above. As parents, it is important to condition ourselves to speak to our NLD children clearly and concisely, without sarcasm, in language which is easy to understand (with specific ideas and instructions). It is only through concentration, focus and practice that I have gotten out of the habit of giving Jimmy multitask instructions or of making sarcastic statements when upset with something he has done. It simply confuses him and makes it all the more difficult to drive home whatever point I hope to make. Just like good writing consists of simple but effective language, so does good communication with the NLD child. Break things down to their manageable parts. Otherwise, the only thing you'll accomplish is increased stress and anxiety for everyone involved.

And by all means don't forget a very important part of the KISS equation—the Silly part. So far, this book has been chock full of advice and some rather clinical sounding notions about how the NLD child's brain works. Well, inasmuch as these brains may perform a bit differently from other children's brains, let me assure you of one thing—they perform very much the same as all other brains in one crucial way: they love to be *silly*. As far as I have seen in my scant 42 years, I have yet to see a parent who doesn't occasionally like the opportunity to be silly right along with his or her kids. So make it a point to be as silly as your personality will allow when you can, to kick back and simply take up space and air. Yes, it is important to help your children, to bolster their self-confidence and try to prepare them for the world and the challenges that they will surely face. But they must also be allowed to experience pure joy once in a while, and there is just no substitute for thumb wrestling, underarm farts, crab races and the occasional belching contest. It isn't always about fighting the fight. Sometimes it's just about existing side by side.

September 11, 2001

It may seem odd to discuss managing inflow for the NLD child in the same sentence as the tragic events of 9/11/01, but it is quite germane. That day was an exceedingly difficult one for all Americans, and it was no different for us. Once we ascertained that no loved ones were involved in the tragedy, our next concern was that all of our community's children were safely returned home and were insulated from the media blitz that was sure to plague our country for the indefinite future. Dave came home from his office in Danbury to meet the school bus because we both wanted to talk to Jimmy and Shawn and attempt to explain the inexplicable, and answer the surely unanswerable questions which would arise.

Appropriately, the school was successful in isolating the children from all forms of news throughout their truncated day, and discussed nothing with them whatsoever. Some parents might be lost, after all, so how could they even know how to approach this matter? They simply fell into damage control mode, locked down the school for security purposes, and got the kids on their buses home.

The following morning, the children and I made our way down to the end of the driveway with some cans of paint and brushes and we painted an American flag on a retaining wall that surrounds a rock garden there. It was a comforting project for the three of us, a show of solidarity and faith, like so many others we had seen while driving around town the night before. Many neighbors, friends and strangers passed by during the hour or so that we were there and waved, somber faced, with a newfound affection it seemed. Most importantly, it was a time that my children could talk to me about this event that changed all of our lives. They could also give me their thoughts, their fears, and their questions.

Jimmy had many of the same questions that he had the day before, probably because none of them had been answered to his satisfaction. Nor would they ever be for any of us. He is, after all, a child with a great grasp of logic and linear reasoning, and nothing that his father and I had said in the prior 24 hours had firm underpinnings in either. "Why would someone kill so many people? Why didn't the pilot fight back? Why did we let the bad guys on the plane in the first place? Will this happen again? Will we be able to find out who did it?"

For the days and weeks that followed, Jimmy created many drawings of planes bursting into flames as they flew into the trade towers. He drew them over and over again, in vivid detail, as if he needed to recreate this disaster to process it, to work it out somehow. At first I was a bit horrified by the pictures, but I quickly saw the worth to them. They were the demons that, had they not been drawn, would have festered inside my son and manifested themselves in myriad other ways.

The only way we could "manage inflow" during that catastrophic time in our country's history was to restrict the types of news media that we allowed the children to be exposed to. We didn't leave the television on for hours at a time, watching the "war on terrorism." We discussed with both Jimmy and Shawn what was happening in the world, but kept this to small intervals and in light language that they could comprehend. Jimmy was particularly worried about when our soldiers were going to catch the "bad guys" that were responsible for flying the planes into the towers. He sometimes acted out scenes in which he would catch the perpetrators himself, and he even used violent language about killing the assailants. While we always took care to validate Jimmy's feelings of anger and grief (which we certainly shared) we also discouraged violent language and talk of retribution. I choose not to believe that teaching violence to a child is a good thing, no matter how you slice it.

Special occasions

There are certain occasions in a child's life which families traditionally want to mark with a special celebration, such as religious ceremonies (first communions, bar/bat mitzvahs, confirmations, etc.), graduations and the like. While we all endeavor to keep our families happy and to include them in our children's lives, we have to keep in mind that the NLD child may react very differently (and usually in a negative way) to the fanfare of these celebrations than will the neurologically typical child. It is therefore highly prudent to either keep the celebration extremely low key or to eliminate these festivities all together, while graciously explaining to extended family members that it is in keeping with the wishes and best interests of your child to do so.

Still, this doesn't mean in any way that the milestone should go unnoticed—quite the contrary. Arrange to have members of the extended family that are particularly close to your child come for a visit and perhaps join you for a quiet dinner out. For more distant relatives or friends, suggest a card or note in the mail, or even a congratulatory phone call to your child. Any of these will be greatly appreciated, while putting a lot less pressure, stress and attention on your child.

Jimmy was particularly agitated when we attended his cousin's first communion and there was a barrage of parents and grandparents flashing cameras in the aisles of the church. From that moment on, he had no interest whatsoever in making his first communion and he became quite adamant about the fact that he didn't want to be bombarded by cameras. The limelight is not something that most NLD children are hankering for, and it makes them decidedly uncomfortable. When you stop and think about it, it comes as no great surprise. There is much to process at once, much novelty in the form of unusual sounds and other effects (unusual body language and facial expressions that the NLD child can't translate to begin with) and the child is essentially put on the spot to deal with it all by himself. This definitely falls under the "You've got to be kidding" heading for the NLD child.

Great expectations

It's tough to explain this one because so many different kinds of events fall under the category. I'll try to tackle it this way: the NLD child wants to experience things the way a neurologically typical child does, we've already established that, and he endeavors to do so. So, when Jimmy became fixated on James Taylor he wanted nothing more than to go to the concert at Jones Beach. When we told him that we had got tickets to the concert, he was beside himself—giddy, in fact, with excitement. He was three years old, probably one of the youngest children at the concert that was truly aware of who he was there to see. A lot of what happened that evening was probably due to the fact that he was only three years old. He couldn't believe that he was actually going to see the real James Taylor and hear him play his guitar right there in front of us. We were in the fourth or fifth row, and his eyes were glued to the stage from the second we took our seats. Jimmy was so wired up, in fact, that he began to rhythmically kick the seat in front of us and we repeatedly apologized to the woman in that seat. She was extremely gracious about it, and completely impressed that our son was so young and so enthused about Mr. Taylor's imminent performance.

Arnold McCuller, one of James's backup singers, appeared in front of the stage and began speaking with one of the security guards. He wasn't there 20 seconds before Jimmy said loudly to me, "Mom, there's Arnold McCuller." I looked at the black man with sunglasses, but didn't think he looked the same as the man I had seen behind James at so many concerts and I disagreed with my son. "I don't think so, honey. He looks a little like him, but I don't think it's Arnold."

"Oh yes, Mom. It is. I know it," Jimmy rebutted.

Once Dave took a look at the man, all doubt was removed. "Jimmy's right, dear. It definitely is Arnold McCuller." Not long after that, another security guard walked over and greeted Mr. McCuller, calling him by his name. Jimmy definitely knew his cast of characters, there was no doubt about it.

The point to all of this is coming, so stick with me. After a few more minutes of sitting and watching this exciting scene unfold, Jimmy stood up and informed us that he was going to go up onto the stage and wait for James and the others because he "wanted to talk to them for a little while." This was when we had to break it to him that no one could go up on the stage, that we had to stay in our seats and watch the performers. Jimmy looked befuddled. He viewed this whole thing kind of like a large living room. We were very close to the front, so he was just going to go on up and make himself at home. I immediately sensed that there was going to be a problem. I pointed out the very large men lining the front of the stage and explained to Jimmy that they were there to make sure that no one tried to go up onto the stage before or during the performance. This totally confused my boy. Of course he couldn't understand the notion that someone would try to steal any of the equipment or instruments from the stage.

When Jimmy asked again to go up and tried to squirm free from my grasp, my voice became a bit terser. Dave and I explained once again the rules of conduct, and Jimmy began to cry bitterly. This is where our expectations of the evening began to be dampened. We wanted our son to understand the fundamental idea that this was a performance, a show that we were coming to see, but he was in his own world, focused only on James, Arnold McCuller, the members of the band, and the instruments. He was so far from the big picture that the rest of the world was literally a blur.

We managed to distract him for a while with a trip to the snack bar (great parenting tip, I know) until the concert began, and then we had smooth sailing, but it was pretty tough going there in the beginning. The moral of this story is, when it comes to big events like this, you have to set out your own and the child's expectations very, very clearly from the get go. Don't leave any stone unturned, any door unopened. As Dr. Rourke so eloquently put it to me several years ago, try to look at the world through their eyes. This might prompt you to ask yourself some questions about how they might react to the event and help you to prepare them (and yourselves) a little bit better.

Summary

1. Excessive "inflow," or sensory stimuli, whether visual, tactile or auditory, is extremely unpleasant and overwhelming and can lead to debilitating anxiety in the NLD child.

2. Common sources of excessive stimuli include parties, amusement parks, anything novel or unexpected, holidays and personal milestones such as religious or school ceremonies, or simply having too many options from which to choose.

3. It is essential for parents to "manage inflow," or reduce the amount of stimuli reaching the child. This can be done by filtering or narrowing down available choices, and preparing the NLD child for new experiences.

4. Keep It Simple, Silly (KISS) is a good strategy for everyday life, a way to uncomplicate an otherwise seemingly complicated world for the NLD child.

Chapter 5

Persever-what?

As long as you derive inner help and comfort from anything, keep it.

Mahatma Gandhi

Lawn tractors, trimmers, James Taylor—these were "interests" that Jimmy had as a young child which we found kind of fascinating. But, given their intensity and the ever-increasing attention to detail that Jimmy demonstrated, Dave and I found these interests to be a bit unusual. Once we became better versed in the intricacies of nonverbal learning disorder, however, we found out that they were in fact a form of fixation or *perseveration*. Perseveration is defined as the continued repetition of words or motions beyond the point at which they serve a useful purpose. Over the years, these have taken various forms. Some have come and gone and come back again, while some have stayed for several weeks and then completely disappeared. But one thing remains true: when Jimmy becomes fixated on a subject, his attention and focus on that subject is keen and unwavering. To try to distract him or get him off the scent, so to speak, will accomplish nothing but to totally stress him out. In short, fixations or obsessions are idiosyncrasies of the NLD child that simply must be handled with care. Following are some of the most prominent fixations we have witnessed over the past several years.

Lawn tractors, trimmers, lawn mowers

This began when Jimmy was two years old, and it was one of the most extreme fixations that our son experienced. In fact, an excerpt from his initial evaluation from the Children's Medical Center describes it best:

Perhaps most noteworthy of all was his perseveration [fixation] on the theme of lawn tractors. During the very first assessment procedure, James asked if we could "draw a lawn tractor." A short time later, on the very next task, he asked additional questions regarding lawn tractors and grass-cutting. His comments on the subject appeared to be stimulated by internal thoughts, as they were totally irrelevant and tangential to the activity or the conversation at hand.

What began with a toy lawn mower (that Jimmy would pace up and down the driveway with while his dad cut the grass) gradually evolved into almost weekly visits to the Sears garden department, where Jimmy would climb onto nearly every lawn tractor on the floor (and there were at least 20). A smile would spread widely across his face as he would handle each steering wheel, describe each different feature or color, and bounce slightly atop the high seats. He was giddy with excitement at the sight of the army of shiny green machines, neatly lined up at attention, their grilles looking like smiling faces waiting for his visit. It was his private paradise. We dared not make him wait until the end of the shopping trip—you know, the "if you behave yourself and are patient with mommy while she does her shopping, then we can go see the lawn tractors in Sears before we go home." Perhaps this would work well with some children, but when there is as much stress and anxiety built around a fixation as there was with lawn tractors for Jimmy, this would be the equivalent of holding a carrot in front of a crippled horse.

So I opted against making Jimmy wait until the end of the shopping trip to visit the garden center at Sears. We went there at the outset, when everyone was fresh and bright-eyed, and spent about 15 minutes or so. He would make his rounds, from one seat to the next, imitating the noise of the tractor and pretending that he was riding each one. The department employees came to know us quite well and were always gracious and friendly. It was never easy to get Jimmy to leave, but he trusted that we would come back next time and never pushed the privilege too far. Thankfully, the display was never disassembled during the winter months.

Oddly enough, during the same period that Jimmy was fixated on lawn mowers and tractors, he was also petrified by the sound of lawn trimmers, known to some as weed whackers. Something about the sounds of these lawn tools put my son in a state of panic, such that he would turn pale and begin running in circles around the house, crying and sweating. We bought him a pair of heavy-duty ear protectors, the kind that look like headphones, and these helped somewhat. Still, the summer months became a time of real terror, especially around the time that the lawn needed to be cut. We couldn't take walks around the neighborhood for fear that we would wander past a house where someone would be trimming around trees or shrubs. There was one particularly difficult incident when we visited my sister at her beach house on Fire Island, New York, and had to make the ten-minute walk from the ferry boat to her house on the ocean. Since there are no cars on the island, we had to pull a wagon with all of our bags, etc. Unfortunately, we had forgotten Jimmy's ear protectors. Along the way, there were several landscapers working on cottage lawns and, well, you can imagine the rest of the story. I ended up carrying my screaming, squirming son the last four blocks to the beach house, nearly running to avoid dropping him. I was fighting back tears as I felt the stares of both my extended family members and other residents of the island, neighbors of my sister who would probably be whispering questions about this behind her back on the tennis court, in yoga class, and in downtown restaurants. I just wanted to turn around and go back to the ferry, but it had already left and, frankly, it was too long a walk.

We finally got to the house where I swept Jimmy into the first bedroom I could find and immediately closed the door. Thankfully, the windows were closed and I could sit on the bed with him, undisturbed, and hold him for a while, his clammy body stiff but tired. We talked as his eyes darted around the room, searching for something, anything familiar, finding nothing. This was only the first half hour of our visit, and we had three more days to go. I had never felt so helpless in my life. We had gotten away from the trimmers for the time being, but it was only a matter of time before another one would start, and the whole cycle would begin again. It put me in mind of a low budget science fiction flick, only it wasn't the least bit entertaining.

During Jimmy's evaluation with Dr. Byron Rourke in May of 2001, we found out that he has a condition called *hyperacusis*, which means that his hearing is so acute that he can literally hear sounds that, to others, might be hardly audible at all. According to Dr. Rourke, Jimmy was actually distracted during his evaluation by the sound of a running lawn mower, but Dr. Rourke said that he had to open a window to hear any trace of such a sound. This condition went a long way toward explaining the boy's fear of sounds such as lawn trimmers and the like. Still, knowing this wasn't helping me deal any better with situations like the one I was confronted with on Fire Island. Only time and maturity helped Jimmy deal a little better with the sounds. Now that he's nine years old, he can coexist quite comfortably with our lawn trimmer, but he still remembers the fear that ran through his body when he heard that sound as a younger child.

James Taylor

This began when Jimmy was three years old, and Dave taped a VH1 *Behind The Music* show featuring James Taylor. We watched it a few times with Jimmy, and the rest, as they say, is perseveration history. At first Jimmy just seemed to be entranced by the music, but his interest soon moved to the instruments themselves, then on to the song lyrics, then to the way James was dressed and the actual sound equipment. Jimmy managed to rig a plastic baseball bat between two toy boxes so that it appeared like a microphone, and he would sit on a kitchen chair and sing into the bat as he watched the tape of the VH1 concert.

When we took Jimmy to the James Taylor concert at Jones Beach during the summer of 1997, Jimmy's idol showed up on stage wearing a blue shirt and khakis—the same ensemble he wore on the VH1 show. So, naturally, Jimmy came to the conclusion that this was the ensemble that the singer always wore, like a superhero's costume. After that night, I was hard pressed to get the boy to wear anything but a blue, button-down shirt and khaki pants. Trouble was, he only had one pair, so I was washing that particular outfit an awful lot during the week. There were times when I wasn't feeling so all fired great about this particular fixation.

On the other hand, there were times when I was. Like every single time I saw my son sitting on his chair with his toy guitar singing "Mexico" or "Shed A Little Light" to his heart's content, his face peaceful and happy, "in the zone" as Dave and I liked to refer to it.

Carlos Vega

Again, an offshoot of the James Taylor phase, Jimmy became enthralled with Carlos Vega, Mr. Taylor's percussionist, and spent countless hours in our basement banging away on a cheap set of toy drums. During this time, he learned a lot about rhythm, hand—eye coordination and how much a toy drum head could take before it got a big hole in it. It's a good thing we live out in the country, at a distance from the nearest neighbor. He noticed that Mr. Vega had a tendency to wear plaid flannel shirts, so this became Jimmy's new shirt of choice. Once Jimmy had seen his new idol wearing a black felt fedora during one of James Taylor's television concerts, the search was on for a hat of similar styling—a pretty difficult thing to find for a child (I believe he was age four at the time). I eventually did find something frighteningly similar, in a clearance bin somewhere, and I'm sure the people around me thought that there was a winning lottery ticket tucked under the inside brim. Okay, so I might have been a little enthusiastic, but they just didn't understand the extent of my son's obsession with this man's hat, I said to myself as I walked away from the bin, clutching my treasure, wondering if maybe I had gotten a little sucked into his obsession myself. But that's what I think happens with the NLD child and his perseverations. As parents, we begin to perseverate a bit ourselves on these same subjects by virtue of the fact that we have become conditioned to do so by our children. Okay, so sue me.

The Mr. Rogers shape sorter

When he was about five years old, Jimmy watched taped episodes of *Mister Rogers' Neighborhood* pretty regularly. There was one particular episode in which Mr. Rogers shows his "television neighbor" a wooden shape sorter box along with some plain wooden shapes that fit inside it. Well, bless his heart, Mr. Rogers always made a point to use very basic, homemade toys on his show. But in this particular case, it made my life miserable because Jimmy became so obsessed with this shape sorter that he could talk about nothing else for weeks. He wanted to get up close and personal with that shape sorter and that was that. Now let me make a sidebar here. We're not talking about a spoiled and bratty child who was kicking and screaming for the newest toy on the market. This boy wanted a small wooden box which probably cost about three dollars to make, but the point was that he couldn't control his impulse to want this toy. He was fixated on it and it was causing him a great deal of anxiety. Sure, I could try to deter him, but I knew that it would only cause him stress and, even worse, he wouldn't be deterred. Jimmy was not going to rest until we found a shape sorter like Mr. Rogers's. The problem was, there really weren't any shape sorters like Mr. Rogers's, anywhere. And, believe me, I checked.

This is when, as parents, we had to get creative. Dave called the local cigar shop and asked if they had any cigar boxes hanging around that they would be willing to part with. He explained that he wanted to make a toy with his son, and they were only too happy to donate one or two. Once we got the boxes, Dave thoroughly sanded one and then he and Jimmy studied the videotape and marked the top of the box with pencil to make the shapes look the same as those on Mr. Rogers's box. Then, with a jigsaw and heaps of patience, Dave carved the shapes out of the top and then took some wooden blocks and carved them to match the openings and, voilà! The undertaking turned out to be a wonderful project for Jimmy and his dad. Our son was ecstatic and exceedingly proud, Dave and I were relieved, and another perseveration chapter was successfully closed. It was a good long while before you would see Jimmy without his shape sorter in tow, and he beamed when he could show someone his new toy and say that his dad made it. In short, there were a lot of pretty cool dividends that sprouted out of that little cigar box.

Mr. Bird

When our daughter Shawn was six months old, she had a small stuffed toucan which we named Mr. Bird. On one excursion to the mall, Mr. Bird somehow made his way out of the stroller and onto the mall floor, never to be found again. Jimmy felt this loss particularly hard, although he never really showed any interest in the toy before that day. For some reason, he started to ask many questions about Mr. Bird, and he seemed particularly taken by some photos I found of his sister holding the toy. He began to ask if we could try to find another one—first casually, then a bit more seriously. Dave and I knew what we were in for because we had been through these searches before, and, with Jimmy, there was no getting around the details. It was either an exact match or it wasn't, and there was no margin for error. So, I started looking on the internet for stuffed toucan birds. I checked the Beanie Baby® collection. I checked eBay. There wasn't a boutique, toy store, department store, or any type of store for that matter, that I didn't check, but Mr. Bird was just not to be found. I finally remembered that the bird was a goodie bag gift from a child's birthday party. I called the child's mother and asked where she got the birds, but she couldn't remember. I eventually realized that this frenetic search wasn't healthy for me, nor was it a particularly good example to set for my son, so we once again went the creative route. I took Jimmy to the fabric store and I let him pick out some fleece in the colors that he liked and told him that I would make a stuffed toucan bird for him. Not being much of a seamstress myself, I thought this would be an adventure for both of us. It was. Several days, tries and a few bad words later, we had a Mr. Bird that Jimmy loved and that we were both pretty proud of. I then made a stuffed horse for Shawn because, darn it, I felt like I could do just about anything with that sewing machine and, more importantly, I felt like my daughter needed to see me jump through a few hoops for her as well.

Microwave

Jimmy called it a "micro*mave*" and he just couldn't get enough of it—the microwave oven. The problem was, he was only two years old, and the microwave was mounted over the stove, so he had to either be held up by a grown up (usually me) or he had to be standing on a chair reaching over the stove (God help us) which, we hoped, was turned off. Even then, he was insistent on pushing the buttons of the microwave, and I mean insistent, to the point where he would just about stop breathing until he could press them. So, the whole thing became this ordeal of holding him up, letting him press the buttons, then letting him watch the carousel go around. You also had to let the time run out so he could hear the beeping at the end. There was absolutely no early opening of the oven door allowed, or there was hell to pay. We're talking full-blown fixation here. The focus in the child's eyes was what fascinated me. I've never seen such intense fascination as I did when Jimmy would be looking at the microwave oven. I remember family members commenting that he was certainly going to be an industrial engineer. I was just hoping that he wouldn't set himself on fire.

Batman

I guess, as fixations go, this wasn't a bad one for a seven-year-old boy to have, since it doesn't seem odd to other children and therefore did not ostracize Jimmy from his peer group. Let's face it, Batman is pretty darn cool. Again, it's anybody's guess how this one started, probably from our watching one of the feature-length remakes with Michael Keaton or Val Kilmer. Jimmy just latched on to the character and started to watch the live action movies. His interest seemed more like a character study than anything else because he truly would study each character's movements, clothing and makeup, and would try to imitate them in nearly every way. I could tell, at times, that he felt a bit awkward about doing so, but he really couldn't help himself. Take the Joker, for instance. Now, granted, Jack Nicholson offers a pretty compelling character to begin with, one who could suck anyone in. But Jimmy was so fascinated with this character that he was entirely enthralled with his every movement and gesture. He copied his voice, his inflection, the phrasing of his words to a tee. The first time Jimmy imitated the Joker's sinister laugh, it was so accurate I thought I would fall off of my chair.

We have a software program on compact disc called Kid Pix Studio Deluxe. It's made by a company called Broderbund (*http://smartsaver. learningco.com*) and it allows one to make computer drawings free-hand using the mouse. During the course of about three to four months, I'd say Jimmy probably drew close to 200 pictures of Batman and Robin using the Kid Pix program. He was also given a Batman and Robin animation computer game as a gift, which had the added feature of letting him create actual Batman and Robin cartoon scenes and a complete library of characters, sound effects, and music that he could use to make his own

cartoons. During this same period, he created many fantastic slide shows using this program and also became pretty fixated on the animated Batman movies which included not only the original daring duo, but all the ancillary characters including the Joker, Penguin, Catwoman, the Riddler, Mr. Freeze, Two-Face, you name it. There was much dressing up, making up and play acting the different roles. Jimmy was even trying to integrate this particular perseveration into some peer play time. For example, when friends would come over, instead of just talking at them about the Joker (which was a particular fixation for him), he would dress up like the Joker and offer them Batman or Robin costumes. I felt this was a much more socially appropriate way to fulfill his interest, and it often resulted in a lot of fun play for everyone. Granted, Jimmy generally wanted to continue the play a lot longer than the other children, so I usually had to be on hand at the needed moment to facilitate a "transition" should it be necessary.

The Magic Eight Ball®

This was an offshoot of Jimmy's interest in the movie *Toy Story*, as the Magic Eight Ball® appeared in a scene from the movie. In case you don't remember this classic toy, the Magic Eight Ball® is a black plastic ball filled with liquid, a white cube with various sayings printed on it and a clear window. You ask the ball a question while shaking it briskly and then wait for one of the answers on the white cube to float to the surface of the clear window. Jimmy really loved the sound the water made when he shook the ball, and he particularly liked the different answers the ball offered. His favorite was "Don't Count on It" (which was the answer Woody got when he asked it a question in the movie). For Christmas 2000, the Magic Eight Ball® was the only thing that Jimmy put on his list for Santa Claus, and he was thrilled when he found it under the tree on Christmas morning. He was quite befuddled, however, when he found additional gifts there from jolly old St. Nick, as he hadn't asked for them.

Fountain soda

To this day I'm not quite sure where Jimmy's fascination with fountain soda originated, but it came on pretty strong and it's still one of his favorite topics. There was a short while (and I mean short) where he mentioned the possibility of having a soda fountain of his own, but we discouraged that one, explaining that perhaps some day we could rent a soda fountain for a very special occasion. While it wasn't great that Jimmy loved soda so much, I soon became aware that it wasn't really the beverage that fascinated him, it was the process of seeing the line of labeled spigots at the convenience store, complete with the fancy cups, lids and straws, being able to choose the size you wanted (and, believe me, Jimmy knew every size by the number of ounces that each held), then filling the cup with ice as well as samples of several different kinds of cola, putting the lid on top, and finally piercing the lid with the straw.

A typical Saturday morning might begin with Jimmy ambling into my bedroom while I'm putting away laundry or making the bed and beginning a monologue about fountain soda along the lines of the following: "By the way, Mom…'

"Yes, sweetheart?'

"Did you realize that at Fast Freddie's they have two spigots with Diet Pepsi® which is really interesting because they have one on each side of the ice thing in the middle. They have only one spigot for regular Pepsi®, one for Orange soda, one for Minute Maid® Lemonade, one for Sprite®, one for Nestea® Iced Tea and one for Root Beer, but they have two spigots for Diet Pepsi®. Do you think that's because Diet Pepsi® is a little more popular than some of the other drinks? That may be why they have two. They don't have any spigots with caffeine-free Diet Pepsi® which would be good for me. I always like to fill my cup three-quarters full of ice and then half-full of regular Pepsi® and half-full of Diet caffeine-free Pepsi® when they have it. But at Fast Freddie's they don't, so I have to fill it half with regular Diet Pepsi®. But that's okay. I still like the soda fountain there."

Whew. This was all such a rush for him and for several months it made the difference between a pleasant weekend and one rife with anxiety. For a while, we tried using a trip to the convenience store as a carrot. "After we finish all of our chores, etc. etc., we'll go get a fountain soda." In a typical environment, with an NT child, this would be a reasonable way to go. But with an NLD child, this is a recipe for high stress levels and, ultimately, an unpleasant situation. We had to adjust our thinking, and look at the fountain soda as a way to pave the road, so to speak. No, we weren't spoiling our son. We were removing the source of his stress so that he could function comfortably for the rest of the day. Also, the fact that Jimmy always filled his cups with ice so that there was very little soda actually imbibed made me feel better about the whole thing. We put a little extra effort into tooth brushing during that period.

Bees

Although this one qualifies more as a phobia than a perseveration, it warrants mention because it takes so much of our son's energies. Suffice it to say that Jimmy is petrified of bees, wasps, hornets, yellow jackets—basically anything that buzzes and has a stinger. And I don't mean he gets a little upset, I mean he goes into an orbit of hysteria. He will take off like a rocket from wherever he is and run erratically in gypsy moth mode—fast and furious, with no set direction and with the single objective of getting away. If you try to hold him or stop him, he will use every ounce of energy he has to break away from your grasp, all the while screaming and crying at the top of his lungs. There is really no reasoning with him at this point, although we have tried many, many times to do so. Jimmy is neither rational nor communicative during these periods of terror. He is entirely hysterical and irrational, pumped with flight response and adrenaline and has no purpose coursing through his veins other than to escape and survive. It's pretty much that simple. I'm not even quite certain that Jimmy has ever been stung by a bee, although he'll tell you sixteen ways to Sunday that he has. And, quite frankly, I think that makes the whole thing much worse: it's the anticipation of the ill that drives this poor child crazy. If he had been stung at some point in his life, then he would have some real point of reference on which to base his fear. But, since he hasn't, the imagined experience is left to the seemingly limitless canvas of fantasy that is his brain.

The boys and the bees

Four of Jimmy's friends came home on the bus with him one day to play outside. While they were walking near the woods, they must have disturbed a nest of yellow jackets under the rocks there. Suddenly, the pests flew out from the nest and stung the four friends, but Jimmy was spared. The boys all came running into the house and told me that they had been stung. A few of them were stung three and four times—on their necks, their arms, their legs. I felt terrible, and they looked in pain. I immediately made a salve out of baking soda and water and dressed the stings. They were all terribly brave, but Jimmy was entirely frustrated that his friends were stung. Even more notably, he was freaked that he was the only one that wasn't stung. This was his chance, he seemed to be thinking, to have gotten stung and finally know what it feels like. He wanted to get this curiosity out of his head once and for all, but he didn't get to do it this time either, he seemed to be thinking.

As if a lightbulb went off in his head, my son seemed to decide in a split second, as I was taking care of his friends, that he wanted to have been stung like the rest of the boys. I saw him rummage through one of the kitchen drawers for a moment and then clutch one of his hands, saying that it was hurting. Confused, I looked at the palm of his hand, where there was a small red dot, and soon realized that he had taken a toothpick and pricked himself hard. He so desperately wanted to be stung like the others, he wanted to be one of the stung. I think he wanted to be able to put some of this fear behind him, but it wasn't going to happen that day. It was yet another of life's many ironies that he watched as his friends were stung by the very things that so fascinated and frightened him for so long.

Perspective

If, after reading this chapter, you feel that the anecdotes I shared and the strategies outlined herein have illustrated poor or indulgent parenting skills, then, regrettably, you have not fully understood the concepts of fixation and perseveration in the NLD child. Please read the following two statements. Write them on an index card and carry them around. You can even chant them repeatedly if you wish, inserting your own names and that of your child in place of ours:

Yes, Dave and I defer to Jimmy's fixations.

No, Jimmy is not a spoiled child.

These two statements are not mutually exclusive. The first statement refers to what I consider Jimmy's unconscious mind, while the second statement refers to his conscious mind. When Jimmy is deep into a perseveration or fixation period, by satisfying his need to be near the object of his obsession, we believe we are soothing him and relieving stress in his world. It is not always the need to buy or have, but sometimes just the need to talk about something that satisfies him that makes him feel calmer.

In order to spoil a child, you have to be giving in to the child's actions and doing something that allows the child to push limits beyond where they were set. Some feel this gives him power or makes him feel that he has somehow "won" or "gotten his way" through whining, asking repeatedly, stomping his feet, crying, whatever method he uses. Although the NLD child may do this sometimes, this is not his modus operandi when perseverating. He is experiencing irrational, uncontrolled feelings because of an unconscious need to discuss, be near, to experience something that soothes him. Without that thing, he feels stress and discomfort to the core. We're not talking about wanting a lollipop or a toy because he's insecure or bored and wants to see how much he can get from mom and dad. We're talking about a child who is searching for comfort, who will find comfort by sitting on the lawn tractors at the Sears department store. So, every time you go to the mall, you by God go and let him sit on the lawn tractors at Sears. He does it, he's calm, and you proceed on with your shopping plans.

A time and a place for everything

Part of parenting the NLD child involves teaching him ways to recognize appropriate—and inappropriate—times and places for certain actions and discussions. Fixations are a perfect topic in which to address and discuss this.

Say, for example, your child is particularly obsessed with electric blenders and you're going to a neighbor's summer barbecue. If you arrive at the party and the first thing your child sees or hears is the blender, it would be rather awkward for your greeting to be immediately followed by a litany of questions from your child to the busy host or hostess concerning the speed of the blender motor, its ability to crush ice or how many smoothies it can make at a time. It would be worse if your child took the opportunity to plant himself in front of the blender while the hosts were trying to prepare frozen margaritas for the guests.

The point is, if your NLD child has a particular fixation, it is important to discuss with him the times and places when it is appropriate to demonstrate these interests and, alternatively, the times and places when he will have to control his urges to do so. In the example of the summer party, if he would like to see the blender to satisfy his curiosity, then you can accompany him to do so upon arriving, and then explain to him that perhaps he can make another visit to the blender after some of the commotion has worn down. If you are comfortable with the hosts, you can even ask if you can make a children's drink with your child once they are finished with it. It's up to you. The important point here is that your child learns that he has to control himself in this particular setting.

Perseveration and perseverance

Perseveration, at first, was a very strange sounding word to me, but I soon realized that from this word came the word *perseverance*, which we all know to mean stick-to-itiveness, or being persistent in one's endeavors. This is a wonderful quality which I have always admired in my son, and one in which I think everyone could take a lesson from NLD children. By virtue of some of their challenges, these children develop a great capacity for sticking with things until they get them "right" —whatever that means to them—and it's a wonderful thing to observe. If you want to get an idea about Jimmy's level of perseverance, read the story about when he learned to ride his two-wheeler (Chapter 8). I have watched my son erase line upon line of writing homework just because he didn't like the formation of his letters. When Jimmy is interested in a new subject, he'll go to great lengths to learn about it. He'll get books on it at the library, research it on the internet (with parental supervision), and ask lots and lots of questions. I have learned facts about things I never even dreamed I would because of his perseverance in these areas and, whether it's about fountain soda or shape sorters, it shows strength of spirit and persistence that I would not ever try to squelch. Let your child be who he is and enjoy his uniqueness. You might just learn something.

Summary

1. Fixations or obsessions are idiosyncrasies of the NLD child that must be handled with care. Perseveration, or the continued repetition of words or motions beyond the point at which they serve a useful purpose, occurs when the child is fixated on a subject, and his attention and focus on that subject is internally derived, keen and unwavering.

2. Giving in to the perseverations of an NLD should not be viewed as indulgent, but as a way to reduce stress and

anxiety by allowing the child to discuss, be near and otherwise experience the object that soothes him.

3.   It is helpful to teach the NLD child ways to recognize both appropriate and inappropriate times and places for discussing and experiencing the thing he's perseverating about.

4.   Perseveration, which is a term derived from the term perseverance, results in a greater capacity to stick with things—to get them "right." NLD children often have a great capacity to study, research and rework.

Chapter 6

Socialization

It's a Jungle Out There

No man is an island, entire of itself;
every man is a piece of the continent, a part of the
    main...
any man's death diminishes me, because I am involved
    in mankind;
and therefore, never send to know for whom the bell
    tolls;
it tolls for thee.

John Donne, Meditation XVII

One of the great misconceptions that I see about learning disabilities in general and NLD in particular is the degree to which people unfamiliar with them believe they are confined to the academic environment. Nothing could be further from the truth. In the case of NLD, social deficits are an integral part of the disorder and its manifestations are every bit as problematic as the academic ones, if not more so for certain children. Therefore, the difficulties that arise must be handled with care, consistency and attention.

The social problems attached to NLD arise because a child does not correctly process information about social interaction—the "unwritten rules" that neurologically typical children learn unknowingly just by observing others and subconsciously filing that information away. For the NLD child, social interactions that happen right in front of him go undetected, or he doesn't make sense out of them. Nonverbal communication is a language that these children simply don't have a way to decode, and is not directly taught to them in our society.

Social skills are made up of a collection of subliminally learned (as opposed to directly taught) behaviors, and social competence comes from the effortless and intuitive use of these skills in everyday social situations (Thompson 1997). Early development of social skills is accomplished when a young child imitates the behavior of his elders and then learns which behaviors are considered appropriate versus inappropriate.

The misunderstood child

The NLD child, contrary to what many around him might think, is struggling to "fit in" and to please his peers and elders. Unfortunately, however, these children don't have access to the neurological processes that would allow them to develop the correct behaviors by observing others—that is, to perceive and interpret social situations correctly, and/or to imitate the behavior. They are not able to "read" the approximately 65 percent of nonverbal communication that occurs in normal conversation, which includes body language, facial expression, innuendo, tone of voice, inflection, and the like. Moreover, the NLD child does not understand or observe the unwritten rules and conventions pertaining to body space and proximity (remember comic Jerry Seinfeld's "close talkers"?).

The NLD child has to piece together the meaning of a conversation from the 35 percent of that conversation that he actually receives and processes. A lot of the behavioral incompetencies observed in a child with NLD result from the fact that he truly does not understand what is happening or what is expected of him. He totally misses the majority of relevant content which is being conveyed nonverbally and, as a result, much of his conversational responses don't fit with the tone and mood of the occasion. His attempts at socializing are routinely characterized by repetitive questioning and extremely wordy conversations. Failing to read social cues, engaging in lengthy one-sided dialogues, and acting in a manner that is uncomfortable to others will eventually lead to social isolation and rejection (Thompson 1997).

As a result of this social "misfiring," the NLD child may seem argumentative, defiant, or uncooperative, but he is usually not aware that what he is doing is unconventional. In fact, his motivations are the same as all other children's. He wants to please, to fit in, to do the right thing. But it all boils down to this: the NLD child does not learn cause and effect through experience—he must be taught this verbally. His neurological deficits usually interfere with his ability to comply, and he has to be given very specific guidelines, ones that most children absorb without a second thought, or without even being told. So, while the NLD child's social misfiring might end up annoying his peer group and making the adults in his life think he is ill-behaved or vying for attention, neither of these is true. By and large, the NLD child rarely shows blatant behavioral problems, nor should this child's social blunders be dealt with as noncompliant behaviors because they originate from a lack of under-standing of what is expected of him.

For example, when Jimmy was in kindergarten and a classmate would begin to cry (the audible cue that the child was upset), Jimmy would respond by putting his face too close to his classmate's face and repeatedly ask, in an unusually loud voice, "What's wrong, What's wrong???" Let's review what happened here. First of all, Jimmy was trying to help. He was concerned that his classmate was upset, but he didn't know or understand that: (a) he should back off and let the child calm down; (b) if he was to ask what was wrong, he should use a soft and gentle voice. Instead, he invaded body space because he wanted to have some visual contact due to his concern, and he asked the question in an urgent tone because, well, he was feeling a lot of urgency about the whole thing. His intentions were golden, but his manner was a bit rough around the edges. End result: Jimmy's tact was awkward and probably annoying to the upset child and the adults who were trying to calm him down, but in his mind he was showing kindness and concern for a fellow classmate.

If there had been a teacher in the room who was aware of Jimmy's NLD diagnosis and who knew what kinds of modifications and accom-modations were needed, they could have intervened as follows:

- Reassure Jimmy that his friend would be okay after some quiet time and that the class would soon return to normal.

- Give a reminder about body space and how, at the moment, invading that space might make his friend feel more upset.

- Explain about tone of voice and which ones might be the most appropriate for the situation. (This should all be communicated quickly and by taking the NLD child aside with as little fanfare as possible, but will go a long way in making him understand how to handle this type of situation.)

- Remind the upset child, after he had calmed down, that his friend was concerned about him and let Jimmy see that he was feeling much better. The two children could then interact under much calmer circumstances.

While the next time a similar situation arises the NLD child may not be able to apply what he learned here, a simple reminder may be all that is needed to avoid a repeat situation from occurring. This is not to say that the NLD child will never act in a way that tests the disciplinary limits that have been set for him. After all, he's a child, and all children need at times to test boundaries to make sure they're real. This confirmation gives them security and comfort. It is important that parents are consistent about limits, and that consequences be administered in the event of unacceptable behavior. It is also important, however, to distinguish this from verbal attempts to understand what is expected of him and why. Otherwise, frustration and a meltdown may occur.

The (over)protective parent

Most parents are protective of their children. It's a natural instinct. However, because the NLD child is so often misunderstood by peers and adults alike, they are more vulnerable than most children, and we parents find ourselves particularly (or perhaps I should say overly) protective of them. The social challenges resulting from NLD have caused the most struggles for my son so far, and have also been the most difficult for me to watch. It is exceedingly painful to observe one's child try, and fail, to adapt to certain social situations, such as an interaction at the swing set, in the sand box, or a simple exchange of words at a play date. These are routine and fun for most kids, and are the very situations that we as parents instinctively try to nurture, to see blossom from a distant park bench as we chat with other parents. But for the young NLD child, the parent's role at these settings is one of an inconspicuous shadow, because even the simplest remark or action can lead to misunderstandings among the children (and even among adults) and, unfortunately, a loss of precious self-esteem for the child.

I have lost friendships (which, I suppose, weren't particularly strong ones in the first place, as I reflect now) because of bullying type behavior toward my son which I reprimanded openly. But, looking back, I have not a single regret about the fervor with which I tried to shield my son from bullying or any kind of hurtful behaviors. All parents do it to some degree. I have always done it to a greater degree, and that's because my son's world seems chaotic to him, and I feel it's my job to try to sift through some of that chaos and give him an oasis of comfort whenever I can. Some may call it being overprotective, but I don't think that such a thing exists with an NLD child. That would be, in my mind, the equivalent of saying that you should assist a blind person halfway across the room because walking them all the way would just be too indulgent. Their world is dark, and darkness is a form of chaos to them. Jimmy's world—the sights and sounds of social interaction—is like a battleground rife with anxiety and insecurity, and he sometimes needs to be rescued from the static. If folks want to call that overprotective behavior on my part, then I'll take that label in a heartbeat.

The family affair

Family gatherings are often happy occasions where members of the extended clan get together after not seeing each other for sometimes very long periods of time—but these can quickly become extremely anxious meetings where the NLD child, who is not used to being in the company of grandma or grandpa, or aunts and uncles, can become riddled with anxiety, self-doubt, and often frozen in fear. If we stop for a moment and think about it from the child's perspective, it isn't difficult to fathom the intimidation factor. We don't see these people for at least a year, sometimes multiples of that, yet we're expected to gather in a room for an afternoon, a day, a weekend, sometimes for an entire week's vacation, and socialize, share meals, listen to stories, sit on laps, endure tickling and hugging and touching, as if we're close and comfortable with them, as if we truly like their company, as if we love them. If all goes well we do form a bond and, as the afternoon or day or week wears on, we begin to enjoy their company and do feel closer to these people and, eventually, that bond does grow. But for the NLD child, there are so many impediments that must first be overcome. There's the huge issue of novelty, which the extended family members may interpret as rejection by the child or disinterest in them personally. Of course this is not the case, but unless the elders have been briefed about the child's challenges prior to the gathering (and assuming that they understand and accept that these challenges in fact exist and are not psycho-babble) they may not be able to view the behavior as NLD based and not as a personal affront.

Then, once the child conquers the novelty of the situation and the people they are faced with, they must begin to communicate with their family members, and the barrage of questioning begins. NLD children, who we know learn only through talking and are quite literal in their approach to the world, have no compunction whatsoever in debating facts with whomever they are conversing with, whether it be a peer or a grownup. It does not occur to them that this may be considered impudent because, to them, if a statement is incorrect, it warrants correcting. There is no emotion or offense attached to it. It's wrong, and that's it. Grandma, however, might see it another way, and therein lies the second roadblock in our little scenario. When the NLD child and his grandmother finally start their conversation, he corrects the second thing she says, she interprets it as the behavior of a rude or spoiled child and the plan backfires. All this before we've even had lunch.

So there goes the bonding family experience. Better to stick to weekly phone calls and letters? Not necessarily, but you have to put a lot of planning and even more monitoring into these types of meetings. Everyone has to be briefed and on board when it comes to the NLD child. If they're not, then you may not want them on the invite list. Sounds pretty cold, but so is a meltdown during the melon and prosciutto. No one said it was easy. If it were, I guess I wouldn't have to write this book, and you wouldn't be reading it.

Friendships

When Jimmy was four years old, I could simply invite a neighborhood child and his mom over and the two kids would more than likely parallel play while the mother and I would chat on the back porch. Jimmy was always very kindhearted and aloof, so there wouldn't be any difficulty between the children or any interaction to speak of. I would, of course, prime the other mother ahead of time about Jimmy's disability and the kinds of behaviors that might arise because of it. As a result, I would usually spend the bulk of the visit explaining the intricacies of NLD to my guest over tea and muffins. I never minded doing so—I took it as an opportunity to inform what I discovered to be a society widely uninformed about a disorder that was only discovered within the last 30 years.

As Jimmy grew older and became more interested in making his own friends, it became increasingly apparent to me how his differences made forming such relationships more challenging for him. He observes his environment in great detail, and this includes his peer group and his classmates. In so doing, he will admire certain children and then decide who he wants to have as friends. Unfortunately, he doesn't quite understand that nearly every tasty friendship soup requires a good helping of reciprocity, and this is where things can get really sticky.

Unfortunately for Jimmy, he never really figured out how to nurture friendships, other than awkwardly approaching another child and asking numerous questions about a subject that he happened to be fascinated with at the time. Regrettably, this is not the way to attract the attention of another six- or seven-year-old, and the resulting rejection was devastating for Jimmy and quite difficult for us to watch.

There have been several times when Jimmy would become interested in becoming friends with a boy in his class, for instance. He might suggest a play date, and the child would make excuses, saying that this week wasn't good but maybe another time. Jimmy would then call and extend the invitation the next week, only to hear another list of excuses. Usually, this resulted in Jimmy becoming even more persistent (big surprise). His actions, though they bore the appearance of desperation, were merely the result of receiving the encouragement of the other child, insincere though it was. He didn't pick up on nonverbal cues that the kid was really not interested in being friends.

Jimmy is now at an age at which he is pursuing friendships on his own, and we, as parents, cannot stand in the way of that. We will be there, however, waiting in the wings, in case someone throws a tomato at him. If a situation like the one described above were to occur, we would forbid Jimmy to make any further phone calls to the child in question or to invite him over. We would say that he could have his time with his friend at school, but for the time being that would have to suffice. We would do our very best to explain, as tenderly as possible, why we made this decision: "So-and-so hasn't accepted any of your invitations, so you cannot continue to offer them. You may think he's your best friend, but he doesn't treat you like his best friend."

We would also contact Jimmy's teacher and discuss the situation so that she would be aware of it and head off any problems in the future. Here are some further suggestions of other ways we can help our children. First of all, and probably most importantly, reassure your child that it's always good to seek out friendships, even if they are not reciprocated. If, after trying to gain another's friendship, they don't get the same in return, encourage them to move on. I've been known to express this as follows: "They just don't see how much fun you are, so it's time to look for another friend that will."

If someone doesn't return your child's friendship, you must assure him that, even though it feels bad, it is that person's right not to choose him as a friend. But this doesn't mean that, as part of that person refusing their friendship, it is okay for them to treat your child badly or with disrespect. It is never okay to be treated badly by anyone, even if at first we think they are the neatest thing since the microwave. We must always emphasize to the NLD child the need for self-advocacy, to stand up for himself whenever he is bullied or mistreated in any way. Unfortunately, the NLD child's struggles in developing friendships can put his self-esteem through the ringer, so it is particularly important that the parent be as accessible as possible, while also being careful not to hover over or second guess the child. This can be difficult.

You can always just invite another child that you feel might be compatible with your child. Call it a form of matchmaking if you will, but sometimes it can make for a nice afternoon, and, who knows, it could lead to a friendship. This probably works better with younger children, who wouldn't tend to find it "uncool.' Sometimes, on the other hand, it is met with complete resistance, and I end up in my kitchen with the other child's mother, awkwardly eating brownies and drinking coffee while the guest plays with all of Jimmy's toys in the den and Jimmy draws on his computer upstairs. But hey, if you want to make an omelet, ya gotta break a few eggs.

When it comes to friends, my advice to my NLD child is the same as to my NT child: you're lucky if you find one or two good ones. Friendships are difficult to build, a lot of work to keep, and you have to be a friend to have friends. There will be a few lucky kids out there who see your gifts and like you just the way you are. If you can find them, what a fortunate person you are.

NLD and anxiety

Consider for a moment the most basic form of learning: a baby looking at its mother's face. This is where it all begins—where we learn how to interpret our world: what to be afraid of, what to be comfortable with, when to laugh, when to be nervous, when to cry. Studies have shown that the ability of an infant to "read" its mother's facial expression is well developed by a few months of age. When in a new situation, a normal infant will glance up at his mother's face, register her expression, and respond to his world accordingly. If there is fear in the mother's face, the baby will be afraid. Likewise, if the mother is relaxed, the baby might gurgle and smile. Don't you remember learning (probably the hard way, as I did) that when your child fell and came running to you for comfort, the incident would be over in half the time if you kept your face calm and peaceful? On the other hand, if you contorted your face with worry, the child would almost always begin sobbing uncontrollably?

Children react to their parents' interpretations of events. In fact, the same studies mentioned earlier also found that long periods of a blank expression on the mother's face would cause an infant to actually grow physically ill. The child would become anxious and confused because it could not read its mother's expression.

Okay, so it isn't too hard to imagine how the NLD child feels most of the time, nearly every day. And how is that? Well, for starters, anxious and confused because he has trouble making sense out of the world around him. This is why routine and familiarity are such comforts to the NLD child and why a change of any kind—and I mean of any kind whatsoever—can throw a real wrench in the works.

If you need change, break a dollar

Any change in environment for the NLD child is exceedingly difficult, and I don't mean just the obvious ones that would prove disruptive for any child (or adult, for that matter) like moving to a new school, home, etc. I mean anything from changing toothpaste to new sheets on the bed to sliding the couch from one side of the room to the other. Their dependence on routine and predictability transcends what many of us would consider the more typical areas, perhaps because it takes so much of their energy to assimilate themselves to the world around them in the first place. The point here is that there are many situations that can, quite frankly, propel the NLD child into a meltdown. Of course, it is not reasonable to assume that we can avoid all of these situations all of the time, but we can certainly be aware of what they are and how they can be best handled if they are unavoidable. Let's look at a few examples.

Doctor's visits

Although unavoidable, this is a biggie. There is just no way around these, nor is there any way to convince the NLD child that they are going to be pleasant. There will be unusual smells, noises, faces, and folks telling them that everything is going to be fine and dandy when they know full well that everything is not. Moreover, particularly in the younger years, the child will be subject to a vaccination or, at the very least, a prick on the finger for a blood test. For Jimmy, the anticipation of these tortures were so frightening that, by the time the actual event took place, it needed every nurse in the office to assist the doctor in administering the shot. I wasn't allowed to help—negative associations and all—which worked out well, since I was too upset to be of assistance. Even the minor tactile experiences associated with a well-child physical exam are a lot for the NLD child to bear, so you can imagine the stresses inherent in a doctor's visit if the child is feeling ill.

In these situations, it is essential that the nurses and doctor be reminded of the child's disorder and what difficulties they will have with the examination. I usually do the reminding upon making the appointment and then again upon arriving (discreetly, of course). Yes, yes, all of this will be in the medical file, but if you think the staff pore over the entire file before your kid walks in the door, think again. Then, once you're in the exam room with your child, try to appear as relaxed as possible because your facial expression and body language will definitely have an effect on him. While acting calm won't necessarily calm him down, being uptight will certainly worsen the situation.

Vacations and holidays

These two major sources of upheaval are covered in detail in Chapter 12.

Change in plans

There's been a change in the schedule for the rest of the day. Sounds simple, right? Wrong. You think it's not a big deal that the neighbors cancel their plans to come to dinner because their youngest is running a fever. But when you tell your NLD child about the blip in the evening's schedule, he starts to unravel. It's not that he necessarily had his heart set on having the company; in fact, more often than not, he would rather have a quiet evening at home, but it's the change in plan that throws him off. Clearly, you can't control the randomness of such events, but you can be prepared in the event that they occur (and, inevitably, they will). Instead of springing such a cancellation on your child, it is always better to have an alternative plan to present to him. For instance, Dave and I might spring into action and invite another family of friends for dinner (apologizing for the short notice and explaining the situation), or we'll come up with another plan for the evening. Then we'll say to Jimmy "Unfortunately, the Smiths can't come over tonight because Josh is sick. But the Clarks can come over, and they'll be here in an hour" or "But we're going to the video store to rent a movie." Usually, just having something going on as an alternative will be better than simply an abrupt cancellation of all plans.

Changes in environment

If, when your NLD child is at school, you get the urge to put up new window treatments in his room, you might want to reconsider. Otherwise, when he gets home, you might have a disaster on your hands. The element of surprise is no friend to the NLD child and, when coupled with the element of change, you've got a double whammy that registers near ten on the Richter scale. Prepare him before such a change is going to occur, so that he has time to get used to the idea. Tell him the benefits. Include him in the decision-making process.

People

Be sure to give your NLD child some lead-in time if you change babysitters, teachers, doctors, dentists, or other people that they regularly come in contact with. Don't expect them to take up where they left off without any glitches. A few visits just to familiarize themselves before actual lessons, appointments etc. begin is always a good idea and should be no problem on the part of the teacher or professional.

Summary

1.   It is a common misconception that NLD is confined to the academic environment, when the social deficits that result from the disability are just as problematic as the academic ones, if not more so.

2.   The NLD child lacks the normal capacity to operate under the "unwritten rules' of socialization, many of which must be subliminally learned. Rather, his socializing attempts are characterized by repetitive questioning and very wordy one-sided conversations, behavior which may lead to social isolation and rejection by peers.

3.   The NLD child can be given specific guidelines to help him avoid social blunders such as invasion of another's body space, talking in a loud voice, or correcting others' statements. He should be encouraged and helped to seek out and make friends with those who will enjoy his company and appreciate him for who he is.

4.   While perhaps seeming overprotective, the parent of an NLD child should carefully monitor his social interactions.

5.   Other common social situations that may cause anxiety in the NLD child include doctor visits, vacations, holidays, changes in plans, changes in environment, and changes in the people he regularly comes in contact with, such as babysitters, teachers and caregivers.

Chapter 7

Teaching Social Skills

**What saves a man is to take a step, then another step.
It is always the same step, but you have to take it.**

Antoine de Saint-Exupéry

You might remember in the early part of the book where I reminisce about Jimmy's wanderings during his third birthday party. He was completely oblivious then, unaware of his presence in a group, much less the feelings or concerns of his peers. Any parent might assume that this behavior is to be expected from a three-year-old, since most young children are self-centered and less than empathetic. True. But this behavior continued into the fourth and fifth years to a large degree and, we learned, was typical of NLD. With time, patience, and consistency, Dave and I have worked toward raising Jimmy's awareness of his place in the social world to the point where, we believe, he has grown into a boy who is quite sensitive to the feelings of others.

I'm assuming, by the mere fact that you've gotten this far in the book, you are aware of the fact that the NLD child faces challenges in social situations. Even if you haven't observed these difficulties up close, you probably know of them intuitively due to the neurological "hand' these children have been dealt. In order to perceive and interpret social situations correctly, the NLD child would have to "read" nonverbal communication, which we know they cannot do well. So, given that the majority of interpersonal communication is nonverbal, this pretty much stacks the social deck against these children from the outset. But this does not mean that the NLD child is destined for an antisocial life—not at all. It simply means that they have to work a little harder at it. We, as parents, can help them along with this, as can many others in their world. There are numerous facets to social skills that can be taught outright as well as through modeling and example, and in this chapter I will outline many of them.

Body space

How close or far away you should stand from another person while in conversation might seem like something that would come fairly naturally to us. Well, the truth of the matter is, usually it does come naturally to us, because we are able to pick up the nonverbal cue that, for example, another person is uncomfortable if we crowd them while talking, and we back up. However, since the NLD child is not able to pick up those types of cues easily, if at all, they don't realize that their proximity to another person is causing any discomfort and they don't back up. Therefore, it is precisely this type of notion that has to be taught outright to the NLD child.

I like to use the "bubble" rule, which Dave and I learned at a seminar taught by Dr. Stephen Nowicki, clinical psychologist and co-author of *Teaching Your Child the Language of Social Success* (Duke *et al.*1996). The bubble refers to a flexible personal space which we all carry around with us. It is wider in the back than in the front, and it contracts or expands depending on the situation. In Dr. Nowicki's book, the bubble has several layers which are appropriate for different types of communication. However, for the purposes of this discussion, let's just say that the NLD child should basically imagine himself surrounded by it, and no one that he comes in contact with, whether it be through conversation, play or standing on line at the grocery store or movie theater, should enter that bubble (which, incidentally, extends out to about arm's length from the child's body). This has seemed to be a fairly easy image for Jimmy to envision, and when he is playing or talking to another person and he begins to encroach on body space, sometimes all I have to do is make a stop motion with my hand or simply use cue phrases such as "body space" or "know where your body is, please" to alert him.

Impulsivity

Where there is NLD, there is frustration. Where there is frustration, there is difficulty controlling impulses. While, as parents, we can certainly understand the source of both the frustration and struggles with impulsivity, we must also encourage our children to work toward finding ways to handle them better. Clearly, this must be a cooperative effort. If we know, for example, that our NLD child usually has trouble controlling impulses after a particularly social type of day, then we can plan ahead and be sure not to overschedule activities so as not to "trigger" the unwanted behavior. The key here is that if we don't modify our behavior we can't expect different results from our NLD child.

Having said this, once we have made the appropriate modifications to accommodate the NLD child, they should be made aware of the fact that impulse control is expected of them. We know of course that this will not always be the case, but the expectation should be made clear. When Jimmy has trouble controlling his impulses to shout or bang his fists against the table or the walls, the first thing we try to make him do is simply stop, which isn't always a simple task. Once we've gotten through to him, the following dialogue might take place:

Parent: Why were you shouting?

Child: I'm frustrated!!!

Parent: Why?

Child: Because I can't find my ball!!

Parent: Can I help you look?

Child: You won't find it either. I've looked everywhere!!

Parent: But why did you need to shout?

Child: I was just so frustrated.

Parent: It's very frustrating when you can't find something, isn't it?

Child: Yes.

Parent: Let's look together, but no more shouting. Okay?

Child: Okay.

Parent: Next time, do you think you can ask for help first, before shouting?

Child: I'll try.

This may seem like a fairly drawn out discussion to make a simple point, but the discussion serves several important purposes. First, it addresses why the child felt the need to raise his voice in the first place. Second, it validates the frustration the child feels at not being able to find his ball.

Third, it gives the child another source of help in finding his ball before frustration builds to the point where he wants to shout.

Empathy

When an NLD child sees, hears or feels something in a certain way, he naturally thinks and believes that others are experiencing that thing in the same way. These children have trouble with the concept of perspective or empathy—put more simply, the ability to put themselves in someone else's shoes. Now, of course empathy can't really be taught, although we as parents can model this behavior through our own actions. But a lot of being able to empathize with another's feelings begins with the ability to *understand* those feelings, which starts with the obvious task of being able to accurately identify facial expressions. Take note of this excerpt from *Teaching Your Child the Language of Social Success*:

> In any interaction, people spend more time looking at one another's faces than anywhere else. Doing so affords us valuable clues about one another's feelings and attitudes. People normally concentrate on one another's eyes, but other parts of the face also have the ability to communicate feelings; the mouth is a very important expressor—just think about the impact a smile or down turned mouth can make! The ability to read and express the subtleties of facial expression is one of the most important nonverbal skills. Because the ability to send and receive facial information accurately is central to communication, even slight problems in processing this information can cause significant interpersonal difficulties.
>
> It is important to emphasize the development of skills in reading facial expressions. The majority of children should be able to identify and differentiate between happiness, sadness, anger and fear in facial expressions. While "happiness' is the most easily identified nonverbal emotion, our research has shown that recognizing sadness, anger and fear are more difficult and could require some extra practice. A common error among younger children is misreading a sad face as an angry one and then responding with avoidance or anger instead of the needed closeness and caring. (Duke *et al.* 1996, pp.53–54)

There are a few ways that you can work with your NLD child to help them better identify facial expressions in others. Grab some old magazines and have your child identify and categorize some faces in the magazine and then cut them out. Group the faces by type (i.e. happy, angry, fearful, sad, etc.) and paste them on sheets of paper. You can then make a book of faces. I am a real fan of those three-hole acrylic sheet protectors that you can get at any office supply store. You can then put the sheets in a binder and go over them during reading time or whenever you're relaxing with your child.

Turn on the television and press the mute button. Then sit together with your child and see if he can identify the faces of the characters on the screen. It's fun to try to figure out what's going on, and this is a very good way to identify emotions (although sometimes it's tough to keep up!). I find that soap operas are particularly good for this, and you're not missing a thing with the sound off.

One of my personal favorite exercises for identifying facial expressions as well as social interactions is to take my children to the mall and sit in the food court for a while. This is what I call hitting the proverbial jackpot. They're more than happy to do it, because often it involves the purchase of some kind of treat, and it provides a hotbed of opportunity for learning. Within no less than 35 seconds (give or take five) we find ourselves analyzing a situation that is unfolding a few tables away. We do it discreetly, of course. On one memorable occasion, we found ourselves about ten feet away from a table full of teenagers, I'd say about evenly divided between girls and boys. The majority of them had cell phones, which were getting one heck of a workout. Once one would get off his or her cell phone, they would report the conversation to the others. The dramatic facial expressions alone would have been enough, but when coupled with the dramatic telling of this one's conversation with that one, of how "she" can't stand "her" and "he" is going out with "who?", of who isn't speaking to whom, the name calling, the louder than appropriate tones of voice, the body language, the giddiness, the dress styles, it should come as no surprise that this table of young adults provided enough material for a very long discussion between my children and me.

Reaction

While feeling for others is important, it is also essential for the NLD child to learn to *react* appropriately. It is interesting to note that children with social relationship difficulties generally struggle not only with identifying facial expressions, but also with expressing their own feelings facially. So, while the NLD child might think that they are making a facial expression that reflects their feelings, they may actually be making an expression that communicates something entirely different. This increases the chances that the child is misunderstood and only leads to further frustration and possibly alienation by his peer group.

We can avoid this scenario by working with the NLD child with a mirror and by asking them to make certain faces such as the four discussed above (happy, sad, fearful, angry) for starters. Then, gradually move on to slightly more complex expressions as the child becomes more comfortable. You can also refer back to your facial expression "book" that you created with your child (refer to "Empathy" above) and ask the child to copy some of the expressions that he sees there, or simply make an expression on your face, identify it, and ask the child to copy it.

Conversation skills

If you've been to as many parties, receptions, pot lucks and barbecues as I have, I'm sure you would agree that deficits in conversational skills are not unique to the NLD child. However, the ability to conduct a conversation is fairly central to the process of socialization and, given the deficits faced by the NLD child, this can be difficult to master.

I can use one of the writer's golden rules to demonstrate a good way to teach conversational skills to the NLD child: *show, don't tell*. That is:

model the kind of conversational habits in the household that you want your child to use, for those are the very skills that he will learn. If you, the parents, speak to other members of the household in a flippant, discourteous manner, that is what your child(ren) will hear, and that is how they will speak to others. It sounds ridiculously obvious, I know, but it bears pointing out. Show the NLD child how to carry on a conversation at home, at parties, with neighbors, when you are talking to other parents at school, wherever you are.

Then, to reinforce this modeling, you can "practice" having conversations with your NLD child at home. You might even want to set up different situations or "scenes" and ask your child how they might begin the conversation with you. Try different circumstances; for example:

- if you were a new person at school
- if you were a friend they knew and saw at a birthday party
- if you accidentally bumped into them in line at the grocery store
- if you were introduced to them on the playground.

With regard to conversational skills, the school's special education department can also play a large role. For example, Jimmy participates in something called "lunch bunch" where, one day per week, he is pulled out of the regular lunch period in the cafeteria and goes to the office of the speech pathologist where he shares his lunch time with a small group of other children. The children, supervised by the speech pathologist, will focus on conversational and social skills training issues in a quiet, low-stress environment. This is a wonderful way for children, both with and without special needs, to interact in a small group setting and learn much needed skills that will help them both in and out of school.

Play dates

The author Garrison Keillor once said, "Just because you sleep in a garage, that doesn't make you a Chevy." Well, this is how I started to feel about play dates. Let me explain. I'd invite other kids over, hoping that by doing so, some magical, chemical, metaphysical social reaction would happen between Jimmy and this child that would make them friends, soul mates, and eventually buddies. The child came over; he played with Jimmy's toys while my son played by himself or talked about lawn tractors or trimmers or whatever the latest thing was, until the other child simply tired of it and asked to go home. And that was it.

I soon gave up on the Mary Poppins version of play dating and returned to the down-to-earth version where intervention was the name of the game, literally. Play dates can be a good idea if they are handled correctly. In general, I find that a one-on-one arrangement works best because it eliminates the possibility of the two invitees going off together and leaving the NLD child out all together. But keep in mind that you cannot expect to greet your child's guest, pat them both on the head and then go off and do other things for the next two hours. Forget it. Consider yourself engaged for as long as that child is at your house. The play date must be supervised, albeit discreetly, and you must be prepared to cue your child if the pair begins to "drift" or if your child wanders off and stops communicating with his guest.

When and if this happens you might want to casually pass by and ask what they're up to. If you get a blind stare from your guest, it's time to intervene and arrange some activities for the pair. If not, of course leave well enough alone, but stay close by and keep an ear out for comments of disdain from either party.

Hospitality

Play dates are also an excellent opportunity for the NLD child to hone some of his social skills in the arena of offering hospitality. When a guest arrives, the child should welcome the guest, introduce him/her to any siblings and ask if he/she would like anything to drink or eat before they set off to play. Since we have a very playful dog and a not-so-friendly cat in our house, Jimmy gives any guest a little run-down on the pet situation and asks if his guest has any fear of animals. He usually then shows them to the playroom, and this is when we part company for a while and I give the two some privacy.

Hospitality skills can also be practiced when we parents have guests in the home. If, for instance, Dave and I have a dinner party or family gathering, we encourage Jimmy to help us serve appetizers or desserts—a task he can handle that also gives him a sense of accomplishment while allowing him to have direct contact with the adults. In this way, he develops wonderful interactive skills, eye contact, manners and confidence, and is encouraged to stay in the room with us during a time when he might otherwise retreat to his bedroom!

Social judgment

This is an area that parents of all children must concern themselves with, but parents of NLD children have to be a bit more focused because, since our kids don't pick up innuendo like NT children, they don't intuitively learn the language of social judgment by themselves. They are ill-equipped to protect themselves against such things as sexual abuse and/or harassment by others. It is important that these children understand the more serious social judgment issues such as (to name just a few):

- what is and isn't appropriate behavior (to be displayed *by* your child and *toward* your child)

- what type of discussions are okay in public and what aren't

- guidelines for types of touching for different types of relationships.

These are uncomfortable subjects no matter what type of child we're dealing with. In the case of the NLD child, however, we as parents need to give some very explicit instructions. Our children are simply not equipped with the kinds of tools necessary to make intuitive judgment calls if faced with such dilemmas. But, if these questions are raised and discussed directly with them ahead of time, many potentially stressful situations can be avoided.

So pull up a chair with your NLD child and have a good long chat about social judgment issues. Bring snacks, tell stories, do whatever you must to get his attention and make him listen. Above all, be specific. In many school systems, children are shown videos or involved in workshops that cover these topics. Make sure you get the information in advance so that you can go over it in very detailed terms with your NLD child.

Appearance

There is a different aspect of nonverbal communication which deals with things that many of us try to control, such as the ways we communicate to others through our appearance, such as our style of dress, our hair style, our perfume, etc. This is called objectics, and often reflects rapidly changing aspects of our culture, such as styles or fashion trends, the kind of cars we drive, the furniture in our homes and the like (Duke *et al.*

1996). While these concepts are difficult for very young children to grasp, I think that children do understand the idea of "fitting in" as it relates to objectics, and it is important for them to do so, particularly for the NLD child, who may be aloof to such a concept. Conforming to a certain style of dress, for example, says that a child is trying to fit in, to be part of the group. With the NLD child, it is important to give positive feedback in these cases, so the child knows that he is on the right track. Otherwise, if the child is wearing his pants too short or too tight and nobody tells him, then he runs the risk of losing ground socially in his peer group.

I am by no means saying that children should be encouraged to adhere to conformity in dress as a means of succeeding socially. Absolutely not. I am merely pointing out that this is one way to approach the maze of social interactions that our children face, and that we as parents would do them a service by providing them with the information they need to make informed decisions.

Dress style is only a small part of objectics. Another form includes body shape and form. It's hard to believe that, for children as young as Jimmy, kids are already talking about being fat or skinny, but it's true and has unfortunately become a focus of nonverbal communication for these kids in our society. Good, bad or indifferent, we as parents have to be prepared to discuss this with our children and arm them with the tools they need to process this information in as healthy a manner as possible. For example, when Jimmy's class was taken to the school nurse's office to be measured for height and weight, a boy in his class exclaimed to him, "Man, you should go on a diet!" As preposterous as this sounded to us, we tried not to overreact, telling Jimmy that at his last checkup, his pediatrician told us that he was perfectly proportioned and healthy. We added that he is making good choices with his foods, getting enough rest and plenty of exercise, so we don't think that the boy's comment was correct. But this wasn't the first time that we had heard this kind of story from school. As early as third grade we had heard similar stories, and I remember Jimmy being excessively worried about it at his checkup. Although I assured him that his weight was fine, he didn't seem to take comfort from my comments, so I suggested that he ask the doctor directly. He did, and not only did our pediatrician reassure him that he was right on target, but he wrote down his height and weight on a piece of paper and showed Jimmy on the growth chart how well he was tracking for his age. He added that Jimmy could call any time if he wanted to ask about it. These kinds of open discussions are vital to keep a child from fixating on things like weight or poor body image issues, and can fend off a lot of potential problems going forward.

Personal hygiene is yet another facet of objectics that is important to broach with your child. In the case of the NLD child, this may be even more important since these children often have trouble picking up nonverbal cues, such as someone backing away from them because of an unsavory odor. While Jimmy is too young to have to deal with issues of deodorant, shaving, etc. there are other areas of personal hygiene that we have made sure to cover with him from as early an age as we thought he could grasp them. These revolve primarily around:

- making sure his teeth are brushed every morning and before bed

- being thorough when cleaning himself both when showering as well as when using the lavatory

- proper grooming of fingernails and toenails

- keeping hair clean and neatly cut.

Friendships

As discussed before, if there is one thing that we parents want for our NLD children, it's that they can find a friend that will accept them just the way they are and appreciate all of their gifts and their eccentricities. There are times when this may seem like a very elusive goal indeed, especially when the school year is half over and no one seems to be inviting them to parties or play dates, but we are ever hopeful that with each passing year of growth and maturity, a pal will somehow emerge to provide much needed fun, frolic and companionship for our child. The difficulty comes when the NLD child decides that someone is his "best friend" but those feelings are clearly not reciprocated by the other child.

The "best friend"

Adam was a very popular boy in Jimmy's third grade class. He was handsome, athletic and funny. Everyone wanted to be like him, and most of the boys in the class, including Jimmy, scrambled to play with him on the playground at recess. In fact, early on in the school year Jimmy honored Adam with the distinction of "best friend," and Dave and I thought it was very dear that our son felt so strongly about a classmate. The only trouble was, we assumed that Adam was returning some signs of friendship to our son. Sadly, this wasn't really the case, but we didn't find out until much later on.

Jimmy talked about Adam incessantly. We heard stories of his antics on the playground, in the classroom, how funny, how smart, how popular he was. Jimmy hadn't yet expressed an interest in seeing Adam outside of school, so we just listened with intense curiosity about this fascinating companion to our son, or so we thought. The trouble began, however, when we suggested that Jimmy invite Adam over for a play date. We thought that he should try to nurture this friendship that was obviously so important to him. In our boundless wisdom, we thought, "Why leave well enough alone if we can meddle, poke the sleeping dog, push the envelope?" And Jimmy was only too willing to phone Adam when we suggested it.

The first time Adam declined Jimmy's invitation, we wrote it off to circumstance. But after the second and third times, we suspected that something was awry, so we told Jimmy not to call again until I had a chance to speak with his mother. When I did, the true story began to unfold.

I'll give a synopsis of the conversation because I don't feel it will be productive to do otherwise: Adam's mother explained to me that Jimmy had called several times and that she didn't really know what to say to him. She felt that the two really didn't play together at school and that they really weren't close friends. Adam was very busy and really didn't go on many play dates…she felt sorry for Jimmy because he had called so much…she was sorry if Adam had misled him in any way. The conversation ended with a clear feeling on my part that Jimmy's calling was, in some ways, a nuisance to Adam's mother. Dave and I sat Jimmy down and told him that, while we respected how he felt about Adam, we felt that the friendship was not being returned. Jimmy said that he didn't care if Adam didn't like him back as much, he still considered him his best friend. We tried to explain about self-respect and dignity (two concepts that we believe feed directly into self-esteem). Jimmy was very resistant to the entire discussion, and was hell bent on maintaining his friendship with Adam, which we really were not trying to discourage. So we decided to stop the talk then and there and merely establish some ground rules:

- Jimmy was not allowed to call Adam on the telephone.

- Jimmy was not allowed to invite Adam over to our house.

These rules were in effect until further notice. He could talk about him, tell stories, consider him his best friend, whatever else he wanted, but the rules must be respected. Funny, though—Jimmy readily accepted the rules. It was almost as though he knew that Adam wouldn't accept an invitation from him. In a way, it seemed that it let Jimmy off the hook. Perhaps, deep down, our son knew that we were right in our assessment of his idol, although he was still hurt by the truth of it.

At the end-of-year PPT, we discussed this situation at length with Jimmy's educational team. His third grade teacher gave us some valuable insights into the situation as well. She told us that Adam was indeed the "big man on campus' that year, but that he didn't really treat Jimmy all that well. Also, she said that Jimmy sort of admired him from afar, but didn't really engage with him directly all that much. So, it wasn't that Jimmy was ignored by Adam—he didn't really try to interact much at all. We voiced our opinion that it might be better for Jimmy's self-esteem if he was not placed in the same class as Adam for fourth grade, and this was taken under advisement.

During the summer, Jimmy made no noises about inviting Adam over, but did ask if he could invite him for his birthday celebration which would take place in September. We of course said he could. Come September, Jimmy started his fourth grade year in a new class (sans Adam) but did not forget our promise. When his birthday was approaching, all he wanted to do was invite three boys to come home on the bus with him after school one Friday and play in the yard and then share cake. One of them was Adam. He invited all three, and all three accepted. It was a very happy day for everyone in the Burger family.

Summary

1.   Since the majority of all interpersonal communication is nonverbal, the NLD child must work harder than most to have a social life. Many social skills can be taught outright through modeling and example.

2.   Some of these skills include: giving others personal space (the "bubble" rule); controlling impulses; correlating others'

facial expressions to emotions, thereby enhancing the ability to feel empathy; and conveying reactions that reflect their own true emotions and feelings, thereby improving communications with others.

3. The child can learn how to be a good conversationalist through practice sessions or role playing at home, socialization workshops available through school or community agencies, and play dates.

4. Since NLD children do not pick up on innuendo, it is of the utmost importance that they be given extra social judgment training to protect themselves against sexual abuse and/or unwanted harassment.

5. NLD children should learn the concept of "fitting in" using objectics, or nonverbal communication through appearance (dress, hairstyle, perfume, choice of jewelry). This can be done by helping them with wardrobe choices, tips on hygiene, etc.

Chapter 8

Activities for the NLD Child

It is something to be able to paint a particular picture, or to carve a statue, and so to make a few objects beautiful; but it is far more glorious to carve and paint the very atmosphere and medium through which we look... To affect the quality of the day, that is the highest of arts.

Henry Thoreau

The first and most vital point to make in this chapter is that there is no magical answer when it comes to activities for the NLD child. It is of paramount importance, however, for his health and well-being (as it is to the health and well-being of all of us, for that matter) that *the child remain active as much as possible*. Perhaps it is more essential with the NLD child because, due to the social struggles that these children face, they can tend to become withdrawn and sedentary. It stands to reason—when interactions on the playground make you feel lousy, it's easier to stay inside and read a book.

Before I go any further let me emphasize that, as with all of the points I make in this book, the ideas outlined here do not apply across the board to all children with nonverbal learning disability. All children are different, and NLD children are no exception. The activities that work well for Jimmy may not work well with other NLD children so, as with all things in life, trial and error is the rule of the day and parents must be prepared to experiment a bit. It is hoped this chapter will give you some ideas and tips that will guide you in the right direction. The types of activities which the NLD child may find appealing include the following:

Team sports

Team sports that require parallel effort toward a common goal rather than interactive effort to achieve a goal may suit the NLD child. These include such sports as track and field, swim team and gymnastics, as distinguished from interactive sports such as soccer, baseball, and basketball. In this way, the NLD child can focus his efforts on the physical activity and his personal goal rather than having to deal with the multiple visual stimuli of many different players, competing teams, different colored uniforms, the noise of fans in the bleachers, etc. that come with interactive sports which are usually played in smaller, more crowded venues.

Horseback riding

This is a wonderful sport for the NLD child, not only for the self-confidence it builds, but also for the stimulation it provides to nearly every muscle in the body. There are many horseback riding programs for children with disabilities available in the US. For information on these, you can contact the North American Riding for the Handicapped Association (NARHA) or go to their website (*www.narha.org*). NARHA is a national non-profit organization that promotes the benefit of a horse for individuals with physical, emotional and learning disabilities. For individuals with disabilities, equine-assisted activities have been shown to improve muscle tone, balance, posture, coordination and motor development, as well as emotional well-being.

Jimmy participated in one such program in Connecticut called the Pegasus Therapeutic Riding Program, which greatly improved the strength in his upper body and really bolstered his self-confidence. Plus, it was really very rewarding to see his connection with the horses.

Hiking

There is a great tranquility that comes from a long walk in the woods, and I have found that, as the parent of an NLD child, any opportunity for tranquility with my child, not to mention while engaging in some form of physical activity, should be embraced with the greatest of enthusiasm. Think about it—there just aren't that many chances for these children to walk along, undisturbed by the blitz of media stimuli that abound in today's world, in a serene backdrop of trees, rocks, flora and fauna, while talking to the undivided and attentive audience of one or both of their parents.

If you're as fortunate as we are and live near a 200-acre nature reserve, then hiking is a pretty convenient option. But you don't need 200 acres. You don't even need two acres to have a darn good hike with your child. Walking in circles works just fine—I've done it plenty of times myself. The point is to get outside in the fresh air with your kid, and to give him some quiet time with you while doing it. You'll be amazed at some of the great conversations that can pop up while you're sitting on a rock, looking down at a pond full of leaves or lily pads. It's just another opportunity to learn about each other; for your child to understand that there is plenty of time to talk to you and for you to listen. Sometimes we even climb one of the rock formations there and scare ourselves a little. But we hold hands and Jimmy talks the whole way up and the whole way down.

Shooting hoops

We are basketball fans in this house, so Jimmy and I spend a lot of time shooting hoops in the driveway and talking about the school day. I find this a good way to keep connected with my son, share a physical interest and make him think I'm a cool mom (when I make the occasional basket, that is, and maybe even when I don't). Everyone wins. And, by the way, there's something about shooting the basketball in the driveway. Maybe it's the sound of the ball against the asphalt or the smack as it hits the backboard, or maybe it's the feeling you get when it finally swooshes through the net, and Jimmy says "Nice one, Mom!" But being out there is just as fun for me as it is for him. I'm even getting a pretty decent lay-up shot.

Music

When Jimmy was younger, he showed a keen interest in music (refer to Chapter 5 and his fixation on James Taylor, guitar and drums). His interest in this area of creative arts has since waned and, although I have tried to encourage him, he does not want to pursue it. However, if there were any interest shown I would try to nurture this. Besides the obvious benefits of music on an educational level as well as the gross and fine motor skills it enhances, playing an instrument can also help the NLD child build self-esteem, exercise self-expression and (depending on the school music program) build social skills.

Playground

The playground is a good idea because we take Jimmy's sister Shawn along and it becomes a family activity. It can also be an opportunity to run into school friends (socialization!) or to meet new children (we've traded a few phone numbers for future play dates). But remember, it isn't quite as successful a venture if the parents sit on a park bench while the children are left to their own devices, particularly in the case of the NLD child. Since many of today's playgrounds are equipped with very elaborate, maze-like jungle gyms, a child may find himself quite overwhelmed and even frightened by the vastness of the play area, therefore choosing to sit on the sidelines and do nothing or wander off. Needless to say, you have to keep an eagle eye on your children in these places because there are myriad nooks and crannies where they can disappear. So, consider climbing on the equipment yourself with the kids to instill confidence in them and keep a watch over them at the same time.

Just one more rock

At one of our playgrounds, there is a little bridge that goes over a small creek with a gravel bank. A year ago, Jimmy had a particular love for tossing small pieces of gravel in the water. Each time we went to the playground we found ourselves spending untold amounts of time at that bank while Jimmy picked up small rocks and tossed them in the water. He kept inching his way closer and closer to the water because he wanted to get "this rock" and "that rock," and "just one more rock, PLEASE????" I kept pleading with Jimmy to be careful because I was worried that he might lose his footing and fall in. He resisted holding my hand so vehemently, however, that I finally just left him alone. Well, as I would have predicted, he reached a little too far to get that one last rock, his foot slipped, and he fell sideways right into the stream of cold water—splash! He was so stunned he just looked at me with his mouth agape, still sideways flat down in the stream. I didn't rush to pick him up, though. I stood there for a second, hovered over him, my hand covering my mouth. Several other mothers were watching me, silent and stunned. Then I let out a loud laugh, and I mean loud. Seconds later, Jimmy joined right in, as did the rest of the onlookers. I pulled him out of the stream, and he was one cold, wet, happy boy. We talk about that one to this day.

Swimming

This is a great activity, whether or not it involves participation on a team. Jimmy loves being in the water, although it took him a while to adjust to the feeling of having his face underneath it. Once he did, there was no turning back. We took him to swimming lessons when he was three years old, but this was before he was diagnosed with NLD. At that time, it was clear that he was having attention difficulties, and he really didn't get much out of the class, other than some play time with mom or dad in the water. Once we did get his diagnosis, we were so focused on other things that swimming skills hardly entered our minds. We took him to the community pool during the summer to cool off, and he really taught himself to dunk under the water. Then, as he grew older, he would go into the pool with his school friends and try to imitate what they were doing. In this way, he learned to jump into the water, blow out through his nose and, eventually, dive off the diving board. He has not yet taken formal swimming lessons, but he thoroughly enjoys being in a swimming pool, and knows what the basic pool safety rules are.

Jimmy also loves to be in the ocean, which is an entirely different experience for him. While there, he chooses to wear a swim mask because it makes him feel secure when the big waves crash into his face. Still, he has no fear of diving under the water, which I find fascinating given his intermittent tendency toward tactile defensiveness (meaning sensitivity toward the feeling of things touching him). Dave and I have enjoyed many hours of wave riding with Jimmy, some with a boogie board, some without, but always with the same result: a wide, wet smile and grateful hug from our boy. What joy there is in that. Even if you have to freeze your fool head off.

Bike riding

The young NLD child is usually a late bloomer when it comes to bike riding because of the range of skills that this activity requires: *propelling* the body forward by pedaling *plus steering* the bicycle left and right *plus braking* by pressing back on the pedal.

That's a lot for the NLD brain and body to concentrate on at once. These children always seem to do much better on a scooter-type toy that they can sit on and push themselves forward with both feet at once. We bought one for Jimmy when he was age two (called a Cappy Coaster®) and Jimmy rode on that thing until he finally got so big that it was scraping the tips off of his shoes.

Still, biking is a wonderful exercise to pursue, and Jimmy wanted to pursue it. He tried to ride a tricycle, although it was very difficult for him. He eventually did better at it and was getting up and down the driveway pretty well. He wanted to ride a two-wheeler, so we got him one and put training wheels on it. He wanted to take the training wheels off, but we told him he couldn't do that yet. Jimmy kept asking, "When, when?" We told him he would have to wait until his sixth birthday.

The bicycle birthday

When Jimmy's sixth birthday finally came, it struck me that he assumed some magical transformation would occur to make him able to ride his two-wheeler without the aid of the training wheels. I remember the excitement on his face early in the morning when he exclaimed, "Now I'll be able to ride my two-wheeler!' and how my heart fell because I knew what was going to happen as soon as he tried to ride that bike.

I tried to explain how it was going to take practice, that these things didn't happen overnight, but he was already clipping on his helmet and climbing up on the bike. Before I could say "bombs away,' Jimmy was fishtailing out of the garage and had taken a nosedive into the grass. He rose from the bike, a look of disbelief spreading across his face along with tears.

Then we made a deal. "The only way this is going to work," I said, "is if we practice this thing together."

There is no word in the English language that my son hates more than practice. "MOM!" he shouted.

"I hate shouting!" I shouted back, knowing it probably wasn't the best idea, but it at least got a smile. I continued. "Get back on the bike," I urged, "and I'll hold you up. Then I'll push you along until you get your balance. Then I'll give you a big push towards the grass. When I let go, start pedaling as fast as you can toward the grass. That way, if you fall, it won't hurt so much. Deal?"

He seemed to like the plan. "We'll do this every hour until you can pedal by yourself for a while on the grass. Then we'll know you can do it on the driveway, right?"

He nodded. I wasn't sure if it would work, but I knew that it would keep his attention for the better part of his birthday, and that was worth a try. It was 8 o'clock in the morning. We did this every hour on the hour. He fell a lot, cried some, laughed some more. By 4 o'clock that afternoon, Jimmy was riding his two-wheeler up and down the driveway. He had a few scratches and scrapes and I was a little sore across the back, but we were both pretty proud—and surprised—by what we had accomplished as a team, all because he was so determined, perseverant, and stubborn. That was a birthday neither of us will soon forget.

Running

Oh yes, and there's no substitute for a good ol' jog down the road. I don't believe in starting this when a child is too young, because I don't think the joints and muscles are ready to bear that kind of pounding. But at nine years old, Jimmy can do a little running with his dad on a padded track at the high school and have a good time. His dad can do his usual run, and Jimmy can go around a few times and then sit and watch, or play, or cheer his dad on, or bring along a book. Any way you slice it, it's a good outing. Sometimes running even comes in handy around the house—and I mean literally around the house. Like the time I was in the backyard weeding, and Jimmy persisted in telling me how bored he was—his way of telling me that he wanted me to stop working in the yard and play with him. I told him that if I stopped working in the yard it would look terrible, so he would have to be patient. He said he didn't feel like being patient. I said I understood that, but that I had to keep weeding. He asked me what he should do. I said, "Why don't you run around the yard 18 times?" I was half joking when I said it. But, consistent with the working of the NLD brain, Jimmy took me at my word. He began running around the yard, and finally completed 18 circles around it, red faced and proud. And by then, much to his delight, I had finished my weeding.

Ice skating

When there is finally enough snow on the ground to build a snowman or go to the local sledding hill for a ride, you've got all kinds of activities right at your fingertips. Ice skating is one wintertime activity that is fun for the family and great exercise to boot. Speaking of boots, however, my personal favorite winter sport is cross-country skiing, and I think this is a great one to get children started on. In fact, this is included in the physical education program at Jimmy's elementary school (they go out on the fields behind the school and cross-country ski during their gym period) and there is nothing better for their cardiovascular health. Also, this is a wonderful activity to build coordination and upper body strength, which are sometimes problem areas for the NLD child. It's a very inexpensive sport—you can rent equipment cheaply for the entire season or buy it second hand—and all you need to do it is a large open field or golf course. Just pop on your boots and skis, slip into the poles (if you can do so without falling over first, which is a challenge for me at times) and off you go. It's a winner, and it's something you can do for your whole life with very low risk of breaking any bones. Now that's my kind of sport.

Indoor activities

Board games

If there aren't scads of complex rules to keep track of, board games can be a lot of fun for the NLD child. Some of our favorites are:

- Uno®
- Checkers®
- Sorry®
- Battleship®
- Trouble®
- Hands Down®.

Drawing

Even though this isn't a physically active hobby, drawing is a wonderful channel for creative expression. Jimmy began to draw extensively when he was about age seven, using mostly paper and crayon. He then turned to the KidPix® software program which allowed him to do his drawings on the computer, save them and then print them when he wanted to (KidPix Studio Deluxe by Broderbund, *http://smartsaver.learningco.com*). To this day, when Jimmy comes home from school, this is just about the first thing he does to "decompress' from his day. He has compiled upwards of 500 pictures in his KidPix® library, some of which are displayed in this book.

Household chores

Washing the car

At our house, we've had more fun with this one than you can possibly imagine. On a warm summer afternoon, this can be a perfect way to cool everyone off, and get a much needed job well done; not to mention the fact that the kids get a stab at spraying their dad, their mom and each other (and anyone else that may pass by, including the dog) with cold water! Just make sure to set some simple ground rules before you get started, like no spraying at faces, no spraying up close, and no splashing of soapy water in each other's eyes.

Watering the garden

Let's see, do you see a pattern forming here? Well, I never said I was dumb. All kidding aside, I have found that most children—and the NLD child is no exception—like to be involved in what's going on in the house. In the case of the NLD child, however, these activities provide an opportunity for learning. Remember, these children don't pick up a lot of information by just watching routines of the household, like NT children are more apt to do. So, the more the parents point out routines and make them fun joint activities, the more these things will be reinforced with the NLD child and become ingrained as part of the fabric of the home and the family. So, you get the idea. You can basically fill in the blank here with any other similar household chore that requires joint effort, a little bit of elbow grease, and a helping of fun: bathing the dog, painting a room, washing the kitchen floor, cleaning the mirrors (one of my son's personal favorites), vacuuming, raking leaves, the list is nearly endless.

Topics and activities

As I'm sure you can surmise from reading the suggestions I've listed here, there is no magical list of activities that works for the NLD child. Like so many other facets of parenting, this is an area where you need to "read" your child and find out what works for him. Your child might be someone who loves nothing more than going to the mall and walking circle upon circle around the store fronts, looking at the scenery or taking a ride on the carousel. Or perhaps you have the kind of kid who wants to go bowling every weekend and then have a quiet dinner out at the local burger joint, where they can talk to you about the week's events. Whatever the activity, the operant word is activity. What you don't want is for your NLD child to come home after school every day and sit in his room playing computer games or watching television. A little of that is fine, but too much can lead to a hermit-type existence and possibly depression.

When your child expresses interest in a topic, such as many of those I've discussed in Chapter 5, for instance, you can easily turn this interest into an activity that can be fun for both of you. For example, at one point during Jimmy's fascination with Mr. Rogers, he watched a particular episode where Fred Rogers and a friend went to visit the neighborhood recycling center. He saw how glass bottles were weighed, where cans were compacted into huge blocks and how glass was crushed by a machine into tiny bits. Jimmy was riveted by this episode, and he asked many questions about recycling centers, and where there was one in our community. I contacted a local recycling center and told them of my son's interest, inquiring as to whether they would be so kind as to give us a little tour of the facility and answer some of his questions. They were extremely gracious and only too happy to set up a time when we could visit. We went after hours one day and Jimmy was able to walk all around, looking at the tall blocks of crushed cans, corrugated cardboard and see where all the materials were weighed. He asked many questions and felt really special to be invited there, and it was clear by our reception that the folks working there were thrilled to meet a child that was so interested in what they do.

Acorns, acorns and more acorns

Fall is a really fun season for kids. It's a really fun time for everyone, if you don't get too uptight about the whole leaf raking thing. Here in New

England, the trees are breathtaking for the first three weeks of October, but when the leaves start falling on these wooded lots (like ours), the job of raking is a pretty overwhelming one. Now, it's a lot of fun if you recruit the kids to help (okay, beg them to help) by dangling the carrot of having a huge leaf pile that they can jump into. We've gotten some of our best photos in those leaf piles, particularly when the dog gets into the mix. Last autumn was a memorable one because, for some reason, the oak trees dumped a bumper crop of acorns onto the earth. Our property was covered in acorns. It looked as if the Jolly Green Giant had dumped his bowl of cereal out on our yard. It probably would have been relatively easy to rake them up had we done so within the first week or so that they had fallen, but of course we didn't. So these acorns sat on the ground long enough so that they could—yes, you guessed it—sprout into the ground. I went outside one Saturday morning with the idea that I was going to conquer the acorn population, but when I touched the first one and realized that it was rooted into the ground, I realized that I was in for a very long day indeed.

I know you're wondering where on earth I'm going with this, but there is a point here. This is where we parents become extremely cagey. Dave and I called Jimmy and Shawn and told them that we had a very important project for them to help us with. We gave them each a large paper bag and told them the predicament we were in with the acorns. We said that we'd make a deal with them: for every acorn that they put in the bag, we'd pay them a nickel (Dave was lobbying for a penny, but I thought they'd tire quickly and that would be too lean a deal. Boy, was I wrong). I think, at the end of the day, we ended up owing our children over $50 each. I'm eating away at the debt with movie rentals and such, but I think I'm still paying it off. Goes to show you.

Summary

1.   It is critically important for both the physical and emotional well-being of a child with NLD that he remain as active as possible.

2.   Team sports requiring a parallel effort toward the same goal like swimming, track and field and gymnastics are better than those requiring an interactive effort to reach a goal like soccer, baseball, etc. Horseback riding helps build

confidence, improve muscle tone, posture and coordination. Hiking affords fresh air and a tranquil time with the elements. Shooting baskets, playing catch and other one-on-one activities are also appealing.

3. Music should be encouraged because of the educational benefits, but also because it allows creative expression, gross and fine motor skill development and, if done in a group or ensemble, social skill building.

4. Although there are hundreds of activities suitable for the NLD child, the best way to find out which ones will benefit your child the most is to follow his interests and through trial and error.

Chapter 9

NLD at School
Working with the System

What lies behind us and what lies before us are tiny matters compared to what lies within us.

Oliver Wendell Holmes

Once you have determined that your child is in fact living with NLD, you have taken a big step in what will become a long walk that we as parents must take together with our child—but we don't take this walk alone. We take it with each and every person with whom our child comes into contact on a regular basis. Of these, perhaps none are more important or integral to the learning process than those at school—the teachers and paraprofessionals who will be interacting with him on a daily basis, whose influence and teaching styles can and will make a huge impact on his progress. It is essential to become involved in the development and implementation of your NLD child's individualized educational program (IEP).

Some people feel it is wise to hire an outside advocate to represent their child's interests at the Planning and Placement Team (PPT) meeting, but this is an entirely personal decision which will vary from parent to parent, from family to family. My personal feeling on this matter is that there is no better advocate for your child than you, his parent. No one knows him better or has seen him go through more—developmentally, emotionally, physically. No one cares about him more than you do. Of course, I understand that some people may feel uncomfortable at this prospect, because they think it is a gargantuan undertaking where they will have to delve into a whole new world, learn the language of special education law, the ins and outs of the IEP form and the PPT process, get comfortable with speaking in front of a group of people (if they aren't already), keep up to date on the child's progress in an organized fashion, keep neat, up-to-date records and interface with his educational team on an ongoing basis. Well, if you think that this is what advocating for your NLD child involves, you've hit the nail right on the head.

Even if you hire an advocate, I don't believe that abdicating all of these responsibilities to that person is a wise measure, and I think doing so would be a great disservice to your child. An outside advocate is a second pair of eyes and ears, but you are your child's best advocate, and there's just no getting around it. It is important—essential, really—to always keep this in the forefront of your mind and to use it as the foundation upon which you, along with the school team, will build a solid educational program for him. If you're the type of person who really does not deal well with confrontation, then you might be best served to hire an advocate to help you, and to be there as your back-up in case confrontation becomes necessary. All that being said, whether your child's advocate ends up being you or an outside, independent party, the issues remain the same.

How to become your child's advocate

This is actually a redundancy—you already *are*. There isn't any magical process by which you become your child's advocate. But when it comes to dealing with the team of teachers and school administrators that interface with your NLD child on a daily basis, being an effective advocate for your child does require more than just wanting what's best for him. Like virtually everything else in life, to do the best job you can you must make a commitment to the process and, as we all know, with commitments comes the need for a bit of elbow grease. Here are some basic steps to take when beginning your role as advocate.

Keep impeccable records

A three-ring binder is your best friend, and should be your first investment. From the moment of Jimmy's first evaluation, I filed every bit of correspondence, notes from PPTs or phone calls, test results, even examples of his school work and/or drawings which I felt were representative of a particular stage of development. While you think you will remember all of the conversations and interactions you have, you won't. When you keep records in a clear and organized way, this information is at your fingertips and can be very helpful when trying to develop the IEP. Perhaps even more importantly, you want to be perfectly organized if you find yourself questioning the efficacy of the current educational plan and wanting to implement changes to better suit your child's needs.

I have filled nearly three large binders with information and correspondence on Jimmy. Sometimes I will sit and look through all three binders to refresh my memory about the various things that have happened over the years, the progress that has been made, the milestones, the struggles. Before each PPT, I usually review notes from the last PPT as well as the most recent IEP so that I can be up to date on the goals and objectives that we are all working toward for Jimmy. I also check my notes for any recent conversations with the team to see if there are any issues that I should be updated on.

Know your stuff

You may wonder why I placed this second in the list. Well, it goes without saying that, upon receiving an NLD diagnosis (or any LD diagnosis, for that matter), you should make it your business to know what the disorder is and what its manifestations include. But oftentimes a diagnosis will be an iterative process whereby several different evaluations culminate in a final diagnosis that seems to hit the mark. For this reason, it is essential to keep a good record of everything you hear and read about your child in chronological order. Then, make sure you familiarize yourself with the current diagnosis so that you can participate as a productive member of the Planning and Placement Team (PPT).

Get to know the team

Developing a rapport with the members of your child's educational team is an important part of your role as advocate. While these individuals do work together as a group to contribute to the overall implementation of the IEP, they also dedicate hours of one-on-one time with your child. The benefit of close communication with these important folks is twofold:

- You can receive critical feedback from these sessions that can, in turn, increase your understanding of your child's needs as well as his progress.

- You can offer insights about your child which can assist them in doing their job more efficiently.

Make yourself accessible and establish a reputation early on as a parent and advocate that is always willing to listen and work *together* with them for the benefit of your child. Check in with the team members periodically. This is a wonderful opportunity for you to add a personal presence to the process which will only help them understand you, your child and your child's needs better, thus enhancing the efficacy of the IEP. Remember, your child spends a lot of time with these people. If you're lucky, which I certainly have been, you may find that you enjoy the added bonus of real friendships with members of your child's team.

Know when to quit

While advocating for your NLD child it is equally imperative that you know when to remove the advocate hat and revert back to being just mom or dad. You must not lose the ability to sit back, relax, and enjoy your child, and let him enjoy you. While researching, talking on the phone, taking notes and copying articles is certainly helpful in the overall journey, sometimes the best thing we can do for our child is to just *stop.* Stop all the activity and hubbub and just give them our time and undivided attention. There is no substitute for a hug and a good belly laugh between you and your child. Not only will these moments offer a relaxed and special opportunity for you to nurture the bond between you, but they also offer your child the chance to open up and talk about things that might be bothering him—in a calm way and to a calm ear. It's hard to "fess up' to the back of mom or dad's head.

Academics: What to expect

We've had a lot of discussion in this book so far about how nonverbal learning disability manifests itself in a child, but we haven't really discussed what you as a parent can expect as a practical matter when it comes to the NLD child's academic performance. For example, how will your child's disorder affect his ability to do his school work, to learn, to participate in the classroom?

Let's start with some basic information about why NLD is considered a learning disability in the first place. Since all learning requires both verbal and nonverbal processes, the NLD child is considered learning disabled for the following reasons:

- Learning in novel situations is difficult for him.

- The NLD child relies on previously learned (rote) information for learning.

- The NLD child relies on unimodal processing of information, which means that he cannot process visual and auditory information simultaneously. (Thompson 1997)

Because of these deficiencies, the NLD child requires accommodations in the classroom so that he can learn in the way that is suited to his learning style. Having said this, since NLD is not an extremely common disorder, you may find that the educators in your child's school do not have a working knowledge of it and are, therefore, ill-prepared to meet his educational or social needs. If this is the case, you must work together with them to move up the learning curve as quickly as possible by hiring an educational consultant, an advocate or whatever means are necessary to make sure that your child is getting the services that he needs. This is discussed in more detail in the upcoming section on the PPT process.

The NLD child will generally excel in those academic areas which involve primarily left brain functions. These include:

- reading

- spelling

- vocabulary

- recall of facts.

This is not to say, of course, that a child with NLD will never have a problem with any of these areas. As I have said before and will no doubt repeat, NLD children are all different and exhibit different degrees of strength and deficit. My personal experience with Jimmy is that he is an excellent reader and speller, but I can also say that we have read with him consistently since he was very young—a habit which I strongly encourage with every child. Yes, Jimmy has always exhibited exceedingly strong verbal skills, so I think he would be a strong reader today regardless. But I think that good habits need to be nurtured.

The academic tasks which involve right brain functions and which can present difficulties for the NLD child are as follows:

- organizational skills

- study skills

- written expression

- comprehension

- temporal concepts

- abstract reasoning

- problem solving

- interpersonal communication

- social skills.

In Jimmy's case, we have not seen a deficit in written expression. Quite to the contrary, Jimmy is a very expressive and talented writer, which may just be a fluke (or may be something that he inherited from his mother—what a wonderful thought). He has told us that this is an activity he deeply enjoys, and it is no surprise that a child will continue to excel in something that he enjoys and therefore is drawn to. Also, his main love is illustration, and he writes stories because he likes to illustrate his stories (there is usually a method to our children's passions). But the rest of the functions listed do indeed present challenges for Jimmy, as they do for most NLD children. Why? Because they involve the nonvisual. They require the child to organize thoughts and ideas and concepts and all kinds of things whirring around in their chaotic worlds and minds. These are the things that they struggle with, the things that overwhelm them. This is where parents and teachers can truly help or hinder these children. Some examples of the accommodations which we have implemented into Jimmy's learning program are as follows:

1. He will not be subjected to timed tests. If there is a test to be given, Jimmy will take it in an untimed setting.

2. His daily assignment notebook will be overseen by his classroom teacher.

3.   He will receive assistance from a paraprofessional at the end of the school day to help gather his belongings, pack his backpack and prepare for dismissal.

4.   He will have a laminated card with typewritten cues stored inconspicuously in his assignment folder to assist him with transitions during the school day.

5.   Grading on his papers will be non-emotional and only quantitative in nature.

6.   He will receive as much auditory input as possible along with visual input.

7.   Longer assignments will be broken down into manageable parts.

These basic accommodations have made the mainstream classroom setting feel much less chaotic for Jimmy, so he is able to function with less stress and anxiety and can therefore focus on the work and the social dynamics going on around him. Without these accommodations, mainstream education might have been much more difficult for him. Academically, Jimmy's performance has always been strong. His strengths remain in the use of language. Math comes quite easily to him at this point, although some difficulty has arisen in the fourth grade as the demand has increased for Jimmy to explain his methodology in solving math problems. This may continue as the thrust in math moves more toward word problems, where he will have to break down his reasoning more thoroughly and approach multistep problems. His weaknesses remain in the areas of science and social studies, two subjects where he has to try to grasp more nebulous subject matter. At homework time, these are always the "tooth-pulling" subjects.

Homework tips

For the NLD child, this can be a stressful part of the day, and there are no two ways about it. Maybe it's a stressful part of the day for most of America, for most of the world. I'm not really qualified to say, but I know for sure that at 5:30 in my house, there's a tension convention going on that could beat the band. Here's how to skin this particular cat. Of course we can't sit there next to them or do the work for them. I save lots of kitchen chores for that part of the day and do them while Jimmy's working at the kitchen table. I might spend most of the time walking back and forth, but I've made the point that I'm not going to stand over him or sit there the whole time, and I've kept my word. Pillar, aren't I?

While the spelling and math are usually not a problem, when it comes to subjects like reading comprehension and social studies, Jimmy can get pretty stressed out. If the anxiety rises to meltdown proportions, I just let him go and sometimes wait until he's ready to return to it. Or, I might suggest that he take a short break to go outside and shoot some baskets, run around the yard, kick the football, chase the dog, whatever. After he's had a break, we can usually come back to it. Depending on his level of distress or the lateness of the hour, I might divide the assignment by asking him to read a few paragraphs where I know the first few questions are answered, for example. The point is, you can't just throw the book at an NLD child and say "Do it!" and leave them hanging. It doesn't work that way. Helping them with homework is not weakening them by any means. You're doing just that, helping them. You're teaching them ways to manage and cope with their own stresses and giving them tools to use going forward.

Perhaps most importantly, know when your child has had enough. Homework is intended to be a learning tool and a reinforcement of what was taught during the school day. If what is happening at home, during homework time, has deteriorated into such stress and anxiety that your child is screaming and you're ready to pop a Xanax™, then it may be time to wave the white flag and call it a day. There have been nights when I took such an initiative, closed the book and said, "Jimmy, enough. I'm the mother. Go curl up on the couch." I then wrote a note to the teacher, and that was that. Sometimes you gotta pull rank.

The PPT

Preparation and participation

The Planning and Placement Team meeting is your opportunity, as a parent/advocate, to participate in the process of developing your child's individualized educational program, or the IEP. This is not a meeting where you act solely as an audience, listen to presentations given by the school team, and go home. This is a working meeting, where the school team and the parent/advocate team talk to each other about the child's progress, discuss issues related to the child in general and with specific respect to the IEP. It is therefore essential that you arrive prepared and able to take part in a meaningful way.

The Connecticut Association for Children and Adults with Learning Disabilities (CACLD) is a nonprofit organization which was founded in 1963 and is dedicated to helping children and adults with learning disabilities. They published what I consider to be a very inclusive list of suggestions for parents as they approach the PPT (Box 9.1), as well as a wonderful checklist that parents can use before they attend the meeting (Box 9.2).

Box 9.1 PPT checklist for parents

1. Request that all information to be discussed at the PPT be given to you several days in advance. This will allow you to be more prepared for the PPT, will avoid having you feel surprised and will allow the discussion to move on to the topics with respect to which there may be concern, rather than rehashing those topics to which there is agreement.

2. Don't feel that the room has to be filled with every professional who is involved in your child's education. You can request that the PPT be segmented so that you can more effectively deal with specific issues.

3. Remember the PPT should be scheduled at your convenience and should not be limited by the constraints of the original meeting time. If there is more to talk about, adjourn the PPT to another time.

4. Take careful notes at the PPT of everything that is said. It is appropriate to take a tape recorder to the PPT to record what people are saying so that you can consider these things in the future. A tape recording is also extremely valuable if there are later disagreements as to what was said. Often the written notes of a meeting are less clear.

5. If you don't understand something that is being said, don't let it pass you by. Request an explanation. In all circumstances, clarify.

6. Don't be besieged and overtaken by acronyms and buzz words. Understand what each of these means and how they apply to your child.

7. Do not have shorthand used to describe the method of delivery of service if you don't understand exactly what the shorthand means. For example, don't accept a statement that says service will be rendered "in accordance with the XYZ model' unless you know what the XYZ model is and have in writing how it will be used. Similarly, if you want to have one-on-one services for your child, do not settle for the use of the word "direct,' since that might not be interpreted by the system to mean what you think it means.

8. Take your time. The more of your time that is spent on the PPT, the less of your time will be spent in haggling over misunderstandings.

9. Don't be intimidated. If you need to have someone with you during the PPT, bring him or her.

10. Don't sign off on your child's program for the next year until you understand it. You are not required to sign off on the program before you leave the PPT meeting. You can request time to review it, an additional meeting, or further clarification.

11. Relax. Both you and the system are working for the same goal: to achieve an appropriate educational program for your child. You are also both working under constraints. Be sure that each understands the constraints of the other.

12. Make yourself a part of your child's program. Request daily or weekly updating of things you are concerned about. Request that the service provider or teacher meet with you to teach you how to carry over lessons to the home. The day at school is only the beginning; the educational experience continues all day, all week and for the remainder of life.

Box 9.2 Parent checklist for an IEP meeting

Information to be acquired prior to the meeting:

1. Who are the participants?

2. Do you wish to include anyone from outside the school system?

3. What are the topics to be discussed?

4. What decisions need to be made?

5. Have you sent your child's psychological reports, test results in reading and math and your child's school records?

6. Are you able to define your expectations about your child's learning and development?

7. Are you able to define what you wish the school to offer your child?

8. Are you able to express your concerns, opinions and questions about your child's education?

Information to be acquired at the IEP meeting:

1. What are the child's individual needs?

2. What are the child's strengths and weaknesses?

3. What are the possible placements for the child?

4. If the placement is new, when will it begin?

5. What are the goals for the child in this placement?

6. If the child is in high school, will a high school diploma be the goal?

7. Who will determine if the child is attaining enough course credit to receive a diploma?

8. What supportive or related service will the child receive in this placement?

9. When will this service begin?

10. What test modifications should be used?

11. Who in the school is responsible for the child's progress?

12. Who in the school is responsible for communicating to you (the parent/advocate) the child's progress?

13. To whom do you speak when you have concerns about your child's education?

The meeting itself

So, you've arrived at the PPT meeting, binder in hand, ready to be a productive participant in this important interaction with your child's educational team. What now?

- First of all, make a note in your binder of the date and time of the meeting, as well as all the attendees' names and titles (where appropriate).

- Let the different members of the team make their presentations, but feel free to interrupt them at any time with questions. This is very valuable face-to-face time with the people who interact with your child on a daily basis. You should be very clear about what they are doing and how it fits into the overall IEP.

- Don't hesitate to raise concerns you have about your child's progress in school and/or behavior at home. Even if an issue seems unrelated to school life, it probably isn't and could offer some valuable insight to the team and/or explain parallel behaviors at school that may not have been discussed at the PPT meeting. The point is, input from the parents is essential to assist the educational team in getting to know your child and understand his individual needs.

- Likewise, if you feel that your child needs additional services, the PPT meeting provides you the opportunity to say so and explain your reasons for the request. Start a dialogue and, if you have more than one request for additional services, try to prioritize them so you have a basis for negotiation, depending upon what resources are available to the school at that particular time. If all of your child's needs cannot be immediately met with services, you can keep track and put forth your request once again at the next PPT.

After the PPT

Once the IEP is completed and accepted by you, the parent/advocate, you can relax a bit and let it "do its job": that is, let the educational team resume its work with your child in accordance with its terms. But your role as advocate is far from over. Advocating for your NLD child involves much more than simply attending PPTs and developing and studying IEPs. It is an ongoing process of communicating with the educational team—by communicating, I mean keeping the lines open *both ways* by making yourself as accessible to them as you hope they will be to you. You want to encourage and welcome feedback from the team and develop a rapport with its members so that everyone stays on the same wavelength. When an issue arises, it is much easier to call a member of the team to discuss it when you've established a relationship already and are familiar with each other's styles, etc. A call every now and then just to "check in" is a good idea as well or, in the interest of everyone's busy schedule, a note via email. Continue to keep up to date on NLD research, and share pertinent findings with the educational team.

Happy faces, sad faces, goofy faces

One Friday, I emptied Jimmy's backpack and looked through some of his work for the week to find a group of papers with various "grades" on them. Some were percentages, but some had drawings on them, ranging from happy faces and sad faces, to goofy faces, depending on whether he had completed the assignments or not. I didn't discuss the papers with Jimmy, but I was sure that something about these markings bothered me—I just wasn't sure exactly what about them bothered me. I left the group of papers in an inconspicuous spot on the kitchen counter for the weekend and looked at them periodically, pondering the question, "What about these markings is bugging me and, if I were Jimmy, how would these faces translate for me?"

By Monday morning, I had figured out the problem. By putting a happy face at the top of a paper that Jimmy had successfully completed, Jimmy's teacher, albeit inadvertently, was attaching an emotional meaning to his completion of that work. He was, in essence, saying that Jimmy was a "good guy" because he had done the work. Likewise, by drawing a sad or a goofy face on the paper that Jimmy hadn't completed in a satisfactory manner, he was making a parallel judgment. While his teacher certainly didn't intend to do so, he had attached an emotional meaning to the grading of work rather than a simple: it's correct, or incorrect, period. But the child shouldn't be made to feel "good" or "bad" because of it, and I felt, by these depictions of faces, that Jimmy's brain might translate a deeper meaning.

I contacted Jimmy's case manager, Joan Cone, and discussed my concern. She promised to take up the matter with the teacher immediately, which she did. The teacher was extremely grateful that this was pointed out to him, and immediately understood how this could be misunderstood by the NLD mind.

Homework

In the early elementary school grades, homework isn't too much of an issue. But by the upper elementary school grades and certainly by middle school, the organizational struggles that the NLD child faces can make homework time a real nightmare. Dave and I had some trouble grappling with the extent to which we should help Jimmy with his homework. We knew, intuitively, that he should be doing the work himself, but we also knew that he took a great deal of comfort from our presence. He was extremely tired at the end of the day, and the physical, emotional and social demands of the school day made it exceedingly difficult for him to sit down and focus on lengthy homework assignments. Still, it was hard to know how much of his plea for help was just a smart nine-year-old manipulation and how much was an NLD child seeking assistance. We took our question to the educational team and received some valuable feedback.

Clearly, the organizational challenges that Jimmy faces make it difficult for him to work through some of the tasks that his homework present. However, this doesn't mean that we, as parents, should hover over him. Offer him support by saying, for example, "Start working on this page and try to complete questions 1 through 6. I'll be back in ten minutes and I'd like to see that you've done that." If you think it will help, you can do something like set a kitchen timer or have him set his watch timer, if you don't think that will add stress. Use your judgment and do whatever works with your child.

As far as organizing the work itself, we found that by the second week of fourth grade, Jimmy's backpack looked like a grenade went off in it. Not only did he not know what he was supposed to do for homework, but he very often took home the wrong materials or books, or he sometimes took home another student's book by accident. I was making trips back to the school so that he could get what he needed or making phone calls to other parents to find out what he was supposed to be doing for the next day. All in all, it just wasn't working too smoothly.

I wrote a note to Jimmy's teacher, Chris Wermuth, saying that I thought we needed to implement some sort of a system to track the homework requirements so that Jimmy could have a better handle on what he needed to do and the materials that he needed to take home to do the work. Soon thereafter, Jimmy came home with an assignment notebook, with a page in it for each day and a checklist for homework assignments. Jimmy was to write down the list of what he needed to do each night, and then check off each item when he had completed it.

This worked much better, but there was still a lot of disorganization until Chris came up with the brilliant idea of getting him his own three-ring binder in which he would put not only this assignment notebook, but also a pocket folder for each subject. Jimmy puts any papers that he is working on immediately into their respective folders so that everything is consolidated into one central location. This way, Jimmy is responsible for putting just *one* item into his backpack every night, plus any textbooks that are needed. The new system has been working extremely well so far, and has resulted in far fewer frantic phone calls to classmates trying to figure out what is required for the next day. Hats off to Mr. Wermuth!

General organization

Another area of concern for the NLD child is that of general organization. It is very difficult for these children, because of their visual—spatial struggles, to order their world. Sometimes the mere task of walking into the classroom and "seeing' through all of the visual stimuli around them is very difficult and they become anxious and stressed to the point where beginning the day is a struggle. For this reason, it can be quite helpful for the NLD child to have a kind of *cue card* to help him get started on his school day. For example, Jimmy has a laminated card in his folder (not displayed prominently on his desk as that could be embarrassing for him) that has a list of simple cues to remind him how to get the day off to a start, such as:

1. Unpack backpack.

2. Give any notes to Mr. Wermuth.

3. Say good morning to two classmates.

4. Begin morning work.

This helps simplify the task of focusing on the beginning of the day and significantly lessens the anxiety he feels. The same type of cue card can be used for transition times and/or for the end of the day when the children need to pack up for dismissal, all particularly challenging and stressful times for the NLD child.

Bullying

It might be a much simpler world if your NLD child's entire school life consisted of what is specified in his IEP—just as it might have been if my total university experience was confined to the lecture halls. But, heck, it certainly wouldn't have been nearly as interesting. And, particularly for the NLD child, the social engagements that take place during free play time are an important, although difficult, part of learning to find their place in the world.

Clearly, your advocacy and parenting must be tuned into any issues that arise in these various arenas. Oftentimes, what happens on the playground can have a much greater impact on your child than anything inside the classroom. Put simply, bullying of any kind must not be tolerated. Your child's teacher and the school staff at large usually share this view, and will intervene immediately when made aware of such behaviors.

It is therefore crucial that your child feels he can talk openly about any goings on at school, knowing that you'll neither over or under react. It's best to listen calmly and then show your understanding of the situation by saying things like "I would feel very bad if that happened to me" or "Did that make you feel sad and frustrated?" You should then wait for feedback, but avoid firing questions back at him. Remember, this is already an emotionally charged subject for your child. Adding more stress through bristly body language, heightened tone of voice or strained facial expressions will only further raise the level of anxiety.

There have been many days where I have sat with my son and listened to a nightmarish playground tale with a concerned but ostensibly calm face, only to retreat to the basement gym (once he'd gone outside to play) and grunt through 30 push-ups (okay, maybe not quite 30, but you get the idea). You'll find your own way of channeling the frustration you feel when your child's feelings are hurt, but do it in a non-destructive way. Put another way, don't show them how badly you feel. Speaking out angrily about what happened, even though the words are certainly not directed at your child, can be confusing and unnerving for them. They can feel as though they caused your suffering, which of course they did not. It's better to try to boost their dampened spirits and wounded self-esteem after such an experience, not drag them down with your own.

Although this goes without saying, I'll say it anyway. When your child becomes the target of bullying at school, do not hesitate to alert the teacher and other school staff to the situation. Chances are, this behavior has been going on for some time and has affected more than just your child. If the situation continues, and no amount of intervention seems to hamper the bully's enthusiasm, then you're left with only one alternative: *invite him to your house for a play date.*

I have found that, at times, the best medicine for bullying behavior is a little private time in a safe, loving and *fully supervised* environment. It may be that the bully wants some attention and can't get it any other way. At the very best, you can rectify a stressful situation for your child. At the very worst, your plan backfires, you cut the date short and send the little joy home, but now the bully can attach a real grown-up's face to that kid he's been picking on. No time has been wasted, and you just may have taught both kids a lesson in tolerance.

A "clean backpack"

Your ability, as a parent, to be organized and avoid last-minute changes or disruptions in scheduling will go a long way toward lowering the anxiety level for your child. The NLD child struggles with organization, both internally and externally. Placing additional pressure on him because you're late, or forgot he needed a note for the day's field trip, should be avoided at all costs. Keep a calendar, or two if necessary. Pack as much of the backpack as possible the night before. Avoid situations where you'll have to call the school, pull your child out of class unexpectedly or surprise him in any way. When an NLD child is not prepared, even a good surprise, like the pop-in visit of a special friend after school, can be met with a high level of anxiety and confusion. Routine equals comfort for an NLD child, and anything out of the ordinary is just plain uncomfortable. It's pretty much that simple.

Field trips

These fall under the category of novelty in your child's schedule, and it would behoove you as a parent to include yourself whenever possible, as a helper, driver or chaperone. Of course, at some point, your child gets to the age that Jimmy is, when he doesn't necessarily want his mother tagging along.

Standardized and other testing

For an NLD child, who struggles with anxiety and higher than usual stress levels, the testing situation is not an optimal one. Things are out of the ordinary to begin with, so adding a timed situation to the mix is not the best idea. If you add to this a standardized testing situation, which usually involves a large room with a lot of children that the NLD child will not be familiar with, you're really asking for trouble. In the fourth grade in Connecticut, students are required to take the Connecticut Mastery Tests (CMTs), which is a state-administered standardized test. Several weeks beforehand, I was contacted by Joan Cone, the case manager on Jimmy's educational team, and asked if Dave and I wanted Jimmy to be put in a small group, untimed setting for this test, which we, of course, agreed to. In such a setting, Jimmy would be with only four or five children, all of whom he knew, and would be allowed to take a break if he needed to, draw a picture, have a drink of water and, most importantly, ask questions if he was confused about the directions for any particular section of the test.

The night before the CMTs, Jimmy was racked with anxiety to the point of tears. By the end of the four days of testing, he told Ms. Cone that he was actually sorry it was over, that he thought it was a pretty good time. There you go.

Summary

1. When taking on the role as advocate for your NLD child, some key things to keep in mind are:

    - keep good records

    - familiarize yourself fully with the disability

    - get to know the educational team that will be working with him

    - know when to take a break and just enjoy your child.

2. Because the NLD child cannot process visual and auditory information simultaneously, and because learning in novel situations is difficult for him, he requires modifications in the classroom to accommodate his learning style. The NLD child will generally excel in reading, spelling, vocabulary

and recall of facts, but will have difficulties in the area of reading comprehension, abstract reasoning, temporal concepts and problem solving.

3. Homework can sometimes be stressful, but this will improve if the assignments are broken down into separate steps, if the assignment is written out clearly and papers and books organized, and if the child takes frequent breaks to avoid anxiety build-up.

4. The PPT meeting is your opportunity to participate in the process of developing your child's IEP. It is therefore very important that you arrive prepared to take part in a productive way. Give yourself time to review past materials, have a plan with regard to what you want to accomplish, and don't overschedule yourself on the day of the meeting.

5. When the PPT meeting is underway, don't hesitate to raise concerns about your child's progress or overall well-being. Be an active, focused participant, and voice your wish for additional services and the reasoning behind such a request. Do your homework.

6. Keep the lines of communication open: share any helpful information you find with the educational team and welcome information and feedback from them.

7. Your child's school experience transcends the classroom, as should your advocacy. Bullying should be dealt with in a clear and rapid manner, and parents should endeavor to avoid stress-inducing situations arising from their own disorganization such as: last minute rescheduling; unexpected pull-outs from class; or any surprise situations or visitors at home after school.

Chapter 10

Discussing NLD with Your Child

**The attainment of wholeness requires one to stake
one's whole being. Nothing less will do; there can be
no easier conditions, no substitutes, and no compro-
mises.**

Carl Jung

I'm sure there are still parents who believe that it is neither necessary
nor advisable to tell a child that they have a neurological disorder such
as NLD or any other kind of learning disability. I don't happen to agree
with this, because I subscribe to the theory that children appreciate the
truth even if they don't particularly like it. When I take my children to
the pediatrician for a check-up and they know they're going to get a
vaccination, for example, they ask me "Will I get a shot?" I say, "Yes, I
think today you might." Then they ask, "Will it hurt?" And I answer, "Yes,
it will hurt, but not for very long." Otherwise, they'll get the shot, it will
hurt, and they won't trust me the next time they ask.

When I was a child, if the door of my clothing closet was left open at
night I would see ghosts in it and I would cry. My dad would always
come in and listen to my story, and tell me that the ghosts wouldn't hurt
me. He never even tried to tell me that there were no ghosts in that closet,
because he knew I wouldn't believe him and, even worse, that I wouldn't
trust him the next time. Better to acknowledge that the ghosts were
there, but convince me that they would be my friends. I could deal with
Casper. I couldn't deal with thinking my dad was a fibber. And we all got
back to sleep a whole lot faster, believe me.

I think it's the same with the subject of disabilities. Kids want to hear
the real deal, because they find out in a real hurry when you're dishing up

something else and, once that happens, they simply won't believe you the next time. Once they get to a certain age, they will become keenly aware of the fact that they are receiving assistance in the form of visits from paraprofessionals in the classroom — help that the other students are not getting, which can become a source of concern for them. In fact, you may begin to hear complaints about this from your child or comments of frustration because, while they want to receive help, they don't want to be the one getting it while others in the class don't. It can be a very difficult time.

If your child had a physical handicap such that they needed the assistance of a wheelchair, or if they had a hearing or visual impairment, you would certainly be very upfront and vocal with them about the types of accommodations and assistance that they would need throughout the day. They might need the help of a guide dog, for instance, to help them get to their classes, to the cafeteria, the gymnasium or locker room. By not discussing this with them, they would be ill-prepared for their day, and wouldn't know what to expect from the various paraprofessionals that would interact with them. They might not be accustomed to the types of questions that classmates might ask, or the looks they might receive from other children in the school during lunch period or on the playground. Now granted, this might be a bit of an extreme example, because a neurological disorder such as NLD is clearly more subtle a condition than a physical handicap requiring the use of a wheelchair. But the point I am trying to make is that when your child has any kind of condition that makes it necessary for him to receive special services, accommodations or modifications in his educational program, he should be aware of his differences because then and only then will he truly be aware of his needs, and the process of building strong self-advocacy skills will begin.

The unfortunate fact of life here is that, because of the sometimes very subtle nature of the NLD symptoms in many children, the needs of these children can be overlooked or mistaken for something else. In some of the many discussions I have had with other parents, special education professionals and administrators in the schools as well as speakers at the many different seminars and workshops I have attended over the years, I have often heard a similar comment: if the NLD child's disabilities were more obvious, accommodations would be much more easily and frequently obtained and the child's struggles more easily understood. It behooves us as parents to explain to our children their differences because, as they learn to advocate for themselves and understand their own needs, they will become more comfortable with the process of the IEP and the PPT and, eventually, they will attend these meetings and become an integral part of the process of their own educational plan. Not only will they know what their needs are, they will know how to ask for the accommodations they need to implement in their plan and, furthermore, will be able to track their own progress throughout the school year. Included as part of this process will be knowing when and where services are delivered during the school day.

The world according to Mister Rogers

> If the day ever came when we were able to accept ourselves and our children exactly as we and they are, then I believe we would have come very close to an ultimate understanding of what "good' parenting means. It's part of being human to fall short of that total acceptance—and often far short. But one of the most important gifts a parent can give a child is the gift of accepting that child's uniqueness.

> (Rogers 2003, p.56)

Perhaps one of the people that most impressed upon me the importance of being truthful with children was Fred Rogers, one of my biggest heroes. Some of you may remember him best as Mister Rogers, creator, host, writer, composer and puppeteer for the longest running program on the Public Broadcasting Station (PBS) show called *Mister Rogers' Neighborhood*. His real name was Fred McFeely Rogers, and he visited with children all over America each day by walking into a small Cape Cod-style house, changing into sneakers and a brightly colored sweater (hand-knitted by his grandmother) and, in so doing, dedicated his life to expanding the educational potential of television for children.

In fact, Fred Rogers spent his life nurturing children in every way, in making them feel the best they possibly could about themselves by finding ways to fill their hearts with confidence and self-esteem. His show had a straightforward but heartfelt format: he told simple stories of make believe, had "important talks" about feelings, about how each one of us is special, "fancy" and "fine" in our own way. Fred Rogers was the guy that all the comedians liked to make fun of because they thought he wasn't "cool." But he taught us and many of our children what it means to feel good in our own skin and, to me, there's nothing in the world cooler than that. It is these very lessons that we as parents should hang onto for dear life, whether or not we are raising a child with a learning disability. For those of us dealing with LD issues, however, I think the lessons taught by Mr. Rogers are even more pertinent, even more meaningful somehow, because he seemed to truly understand the gifts that every single child brings to the world. Consider this interesting quote taken from the book *The World According to Mister Rogers*:

> Part of the problem with the word *disabilities* is that it immediately suggests an inability to see or hear or walk or do other things that many of us take for granted. But what of people who can't feel? Or talk about their feelings? Or manage their feelings in constructive ways? What of people who aren't able to form close and strong relationships? And people who cannot find fulfillment in their lives, or those who have lost hope, who live in disappointment and bitterness and find in life no joy, no love? These, it seems to me, are the real disabilities.

(Rogers 2003, p.25)

Fred Rogers didn't really intend to go into television. In fact, he was all set to go to the seminary when he graduated from Rollins College, but after seeing some disappointing TV shows at his parents' house, Fred Rogers declared that he'd like to take a crack at the television business and joined NBC in New York as a gopher. In 1953, he returned to his hometown area of western Pennsylvania with his new wife, Joanne, and helped found Pittsburgh's public television station, WQED, and co-produced an hour-long live daily children's program called *The Children's Corner*, for which he also worked behind the scenes as puppeteer and musician. Fred wanted to increase his understanding of children, and took this opportunity to begin a study of children and families at the Graduate School of Child Development in the University of Pittsburgh's School of Medicine. While there, he worked closely with young children under the supervision of Dr. Margaret B. McFarland, clinical psychologist. Fred also completed a Master of Divinity degree at the Pittsburgh Theological Seminary and was ordained as a Presbyterian minister in 1963 with the unique charge of serving children and families through the media.

In 1971, Fred Rogers founded Family Communications, Inc. (FCI), a non-profit company for the production of *Mister Rogers' Neighborhood* and other materials (www.fci.org). The company's ongoing work continues to be guided by Fred Rogers's mission of communicating with young children and their families in clear, honest, nurturing and supportive ways. Fred Rogers won just about every major award in television and education and has received honorary degrees from more than 40 colleges and universities. In 2002, he was awarded the Presidential Medal of Freedom, the national's highest civilian honor.

Fred Rogers passed away in 2003, and it was an extremely sad day for everyone in our family. We lost a dear friend, but his spirit will always live in our hearts. Thanks, Mister Rogers.

Different, but not so different

As much as we must impress upon our kids that there is no one else in the universe like them, it is invaluable to them that at times they feel like "one of the bunch." While it is vital that we advocate for our NLD children, that we channel our efforts in any and every way necessary to make their world more manageable, less chaotic, and more comfortable for them, it is equally important that we impress upon our children that they share a special sameness with the millions of other kids in the world. After all, they're just kids like everyone else, and they should enjoy the stuffing out of being just that. We can and should allow them to understand, perhaps even revel in their differences, yes, but not to the detriment of enjoying a bit of the camaraderie that comes from conformity, of being "one of the crowd," of being kids among kids.

For the NLD child, who often struggles with social interaction to begin with, feeling like "one of the crowd" can be a lofty goal considering the fact that fostering a relationship with any part of the crowd can seem a tall order indeed. But sometimes hooking himself up with just one peer can make all the difference, and it can pave the way to other groups of friends. Before you know it, your child can start feeling like one of a group of kids that know him and accept him, just the way he is.

Self-advocacy

Clearly, as a preschool child, Jimmy was too young to understand all the intricacies of self-advocacy, of standing up for himself. Nor did he have to, being under the watchful eye of a parent or teacher almost constantly. Still, he certainly understood that it wasn't okay if his classmate Johnny grabbed a toy from him. If that were to happen, Jimmy knew: (a) to tell Johnny that he wanted it back, or (b) come and tell Mom or Dad about it. These are both tools of communication and forms of self-advocacy which Jimmy was taught, as distinguishable from: (a) grabbing back the toy from Johnny or (b) smacking Johnny on the head.

Someone was nearby nearly every step of the way, so any situation could be monitored and controlled. But, as Jimmy grew, so did the complexities of social interactions with his peer group. We had to provide him with more complex tools with which to self-advocate in social situations. Oftentimes this would involve "staging" conversations so that we could practice different advocacy tactics he might use with his peers. Oddly enough, this is one area where your child's disability can prove extremely helpful to them. The NLD child's natural strength is their use of language, and this is exactly what you want them to use. You don't want any physical manifestations of their frustrations with their peers to surface. What you do want is for them to consistently *talk it out*. If there is a conflict, you must emphasize: Tell your friends what you don't like and why you don't like it, and ask them not to do it again. If all else fails, you instruct your child to find a trustworthy grownup and seek help. By instilling important lessons of self-advocacy, you will be acting as a responsible and protective parent without being a smothering, meddlesome one.

Discussing NLD

I remember the first time I spoke to Jimmy about his disability. He was in first grade, and Dave and I had decided that we were going to move to another town where the special education program in the public school had an excellent reputation. We hadn't really rehearsed ahead of time what we would say to our son or, for that matter, had even discussed it with each other. "You have a special kind of brain, Jimmy," I said, "and because your brain is so special, you need to be taught in a certain way so that you can learn well. The teachers in this new school understand about your special brain and about the way that you need to be taught, and they will teach you just that way, so that it will be easy for you to learn without becoming frustrated."

Of course we didn't discuss anything more complex than that for the simple reason that going on about his right and left brains, how they do or don't communicate with each other and which functions in his body they control probably would have scared the pants off of our boy. Better, we thought, that we just love him to pieces, keep him safe, warm and healthy and keep his mind alive with wonder. While we will continue to do these things, things have changed since Jimmy's gotten older. He is now nine years old and is aware, for instance, that only he and one other boy in his fourth grade class were called out of the regular education classroom and into a small conference room to take the Connecticut Mastery Tests (CMTs) with three other children in a relaxed, untimed environment. He wondered why this was so. Our conversation went something like this:

> *Mom:*   The school asked me if dad and I thought you might be more comfortable taking the test in a smaller group that would not be timed, and I said yes I thought you would.
>
> *Jimmy:*   [Silence.]
>
> *Mom:*   Do you agree with my answer to them, Jimmy?
>
> *Jimmy:*   Yeah, but why were just me and one other kid from my class put in that smaller group?
>
> *Mom:*   Because you were the only ones that seemed to be uncomfortable with the larger group and the timed test setting.
>
> *Jimmy:*   [Shouting] But Mom, I want to be a regular kid!

You might recall, in Chapter 2, my description of our not so successful attendance at a friend's birthday party, after which Jimmy posed the question to me "Why am I so wrong?" One could argue that, even then, he knew that he had differences. Perhaps this is so, while I would argue that he was more miffed at the fact that he repeatedly had bad times at parties but saw no irregularity in it whatsoever. In this case, however, Jimmy clearly saw the fact that he was being "pulled out" of the normal testing situation and taken to a different room as some kind of accommodation that made him strange, and concluded that there must have been some bad reason for it. While this was certainly not true, he now had more questions in his mind than answers and it was time to address these questions.

After all, this is how it goes when you're a parent: there are no yellow flags telling you how many laps are left to go before the finish line. A thought in a child's head leads to a question—and it's time for a sit-down right then and there. That's it. Period. Put down the phone, the newspaper, or whatever you're doing. It's time to tune in—your child is asking for your undivided attention.

So, when Jimmy told me that he wanted to be a regular kid, I immediately knew that he had reached a level of understanding about himself that he didn't have before. This was a turning point for him, and I had to deal with it carefully but quickly.

Mom: You *are* a regular kid.

Jimmy: If I were a regular kid, then I would be in the big room like everyone else.

Mom: Jimmy, suppose you were on line at an ice cream store with four of your friends and you were all going to order ice cream cones. Let's say that all four of your friends chose to order chocolate ice cream cones but you wanted to order cookie dough. Would it mean, because you chose to order cookie dough ice cream instead of chocolate, that you were not a regular kid?

Jimmy: No, I guess not.

Mom: There you go. You're still a regular kid, honey. You just have cookie dough ice cream sometimes, instead of chocolate, like the rest of the kids. Everyone is different, and has different needs. At the ice cream store they happen to seem a little less noticeable than at school, that's all.

Jimmy: Hmmm.

Mom: The most important thing to remember about the CMTs is that you're in that smaller room because it makes you feel more comfortable during the test, so that you can do the work you need to do without worrying about anything else. That's the only reason. Okay?

Jimmy: [Pause.]

Jimmy: Okay. But why is it that only me and that other kid in my class don't feel comfortable with the big room and being timed?

Mom: I guess the same reason why you don't like chocolate ice cream.

Jimmy: Mom, that doesn't make any sense. We're not talking about ice cream.

Mom: What I'm trying to say is that everyone is different.

Jimmy: Well, all I know is that everyone else in the class is taking the test the same way.

Mom: Do you want to take the test the way all the other kids are taking it?

Jimmy: No.

Mom: Because you know that you wouldn't feel comfortable that way, right?

Jimmy: Um, yeah.

Mom: Maybe you can understand that this is what you need and it doesn't make you weird, it just means that you have different needs when it comes to taking tests?

This might be a good opportunity to talk with your child about other types of differences among children, of which there are many, that force them to make special "allowances" throughout the school day, such as:

- *Allergies:* in our public school, some children must sit at a "nut-free' table in the cafeteria during lunch time, and all children must carry a note in their lunch box if they have food containing *any* nut ingredients whatsoever.

- *Medications:* some children must take medications which are administered by the nurse's office.

- *Physical handicaps:* wheelchairs, crutches and other types of assistive technology are commonly used to accommodate children throughout the day.

Discussing NLD with siblings

Jimmy's sister Shawn is nearly seven years old, but she began asking questions about why Jimmy was going to certain appointments as early as a year ago. She didn't press the questions, but I knew that she was curious and, frankly, I would have wondered if she wasn't. Jimmy sees a psychologist once a week, and this gives us the opportunity to sit together quietly for 45 minutes or so. Plus, the waiting room of the doctor's office has several books concerning learning differences, and Shawn picked up one about Attention Deficit Disorder several times and asked me to read it to her. It was a children's book about a young boy with ADD who was having trouble in school and was diagnosed and then got help from his doctor. I read it to her without really explaining much about ADD to her at all. After I read it to her for about three weeks in a row, she finally asked, "Mom, what is Attention Deficit Disorder?"

Well, this was my chance, and I went for it. While of course ADD is very different from NLD, it gave me just the springboard that I needed to have a discussion about learning differences in general. By reading the ADD book with Shawn, she was able to understand the concept fairly well. Her first question was whether or not she had anything like ADD or any other kind of learning difference. When I told her that Jimmy did, at first she seemed uncomfortable, as if she didn't want to continue having the discussion, but I gently continued using positive language. I asked her if she thought that having a learning difference meant that Jimmy was not as smart as other children. She responded immediately and with great enthusiasm, "No! Jimmy is *very smart!*" I told her that she was absolutely right, that a learning difference means that Jimmy has a special kind of brain which means that he has to be taught in a certain way in order to learn well. She then asked, "Well, do I have a special brain too?"

A note about "disability"

While I'm a strong proponent of discussing your child's differences with him, I'm not all that keen on using the words "disability" or "disorder" when discussing NLD for the simple reason that the child might easily misinterpret this to mean that they're "bad" or "wrong." As a parent, you just don't want to go down that road, plain and simple. In fact, I'm quite certain I've never used either of these words when talking to Jimmy about his neurological uniqueness. I can't really imagine any situation in life, come to think of it, when heavy, complicated language is helpful or productive when explaining a new idea or concept. If you can't break it down to fourth grade terms, well, I reckon you just don't get it yourself. When you're talking to your kid you'd better know what you're talking about because there's no place to hide.

As the title of this book would indicate, I've been known to refer to nonverbal learning disability as having a "special kind of brain," mostly because that's precisely what I think it is. There are times when, living with Jimmy as I do and watching the things that he does, I am hard pressed to see NLD as a disorder at all. I consider it a difference, certainly, like being left-handed or albino or bald. Like everything else in life, where there are weaknesses, so there are strengths. I have seen my son struggle to walk through a room full of people or spend an hour at a birthday party. I have also watched him create pencil and computer drawings the likes of which I have never seen, full of expression and detail, rife with action and emotion. Drawings like these take patience and control, a keen eye and a steady hand, and a perspective on the world that only a special kind of brain could embrace. I have listened to his inspired philosophies on time travel, and watched him solve math problems so quickly that my head was left spinning. I have heard my son speak with clarity and wisdom while I was melting down over losing my keys or locking myself out of my office. On one particular day, I remember actually beginning to scream at myself in the car when Jimmy said, "Mom, let's just calm down for a minute. Why don't we go inside the building and ask someone for help?" "Now why didn't I think of that?" I thought to myself.

The gifts of the NLD child are not just in the compensation for their deficits, but in the very unique way in which these children approach their world. Theirs is a very literal sense, an ordered approach to things that many of us just don't have. Like Fred Rogers, I choose not to see NLD as an "inability" to do anything, but instead an ability to do many things differently. And this is precisely how I have tried to explain NLD to my son.

Summary

1.   It behooves us as parents to explain to our children their learning differences because, as they learn to advocate for themselves and understand their own needs, they will eventually become an integral part of the process of their own educational plan.

2.   In order to maintain credibility with your child, answer his questions about NLD in an age-appropriate manner. Be

honest, point out that they learn differently than some other children, but avoid using the term "disability" or "disorder." Point out that the accommodations that are made are there to help him.

3. As much as we must impress upon our kids that there is no one else just like them, it is also very important that they are made to feel like "one of the crowd" at times. Let them be kids, and indulge themselves in the joy of conformity.

4. Self-advocacy is an important skill that the NLD child must acquire.

5. It is important that the parent of the NLD child discuss the disorder with his sibling(s) in a clear and careful manner, and allow them to ask questions about what can be a very confusing disability.

Chapter 11
Living with NLD Every Day

**Every oak tree started out as a couple of nuts who
decided to stand their ground.**

Unknown

It is very easy to fall into the trap of focusing a bit too much on the
NLD part of the NLD child. I say this with some resolve only because
I have been guilty of it. Perhaps because Jimmy was my firstborn, or
because he was diagnosed at a young age, or both—whatever the reason,
when there is something awry with your child, whatever that may be, it is
difficult to focus on anything else. When that "thing" enters into nearly
every facet of his and your daily life, well, it becomes almost impossible
to overlook it. A very wise doctor friend of mine likened it to an abscess
on the brain. You certainly don't want it to get any bigger. You don't even
really want it to stay the same size. The ideal situation is to get rid of it all
together, which would indicate that you're not letting the "thing" take
over your mind anymore.

The "run around"
We don't know exactly when it started to happen, but we suspect it was
when Jimmy was around 18 months old and on one occasion he had a
particularly hard time, well, pooping. For whatever reason, he went
through a very long period, I'd say three to four years, of withholding
bowel movements for weeks at a time. He would try to put off the feeling
of having to go by literally running around the house until the sensation
would pass. Of course, this would eventually result in constipation, and it
would just be harder and harder for him to go. We spoke to Jimmy's pediatrician about it, and he prescribed a natural laxative to be given daily.

We had to give it to Jimmy in his milk, which we took to calling "chocolate milk," and it was a struggle to get him to drink it. We even tried putting it on ice cream. We finally found the right formula of milk to laxative, but it didn't seem to help our poor boy's struggle all that much.

I tried to find out if there was any connection between the NLD and this withholding of bowel movements, but there didn't seem to be any link as far as I could see in the information that was available. However, when I spoke to Jimmy's occupational therapist, she told me that she had seen similar cases in other NLD children as well as in autistic children. She confirmed that there was no clinical link, but that it was an extremely interesting coincidence. Perhaps it stemmed from the weakness in fine and gross motor skills, or maybe it was the child's subconscious need for control amid chaos.

Whatever the cause, the problem had become a major one for Jimmy. I began sitting Jimmy on the toilet as soon as he began to run around, thinking that this would prevent him from staving off the sensation to move his bowels. He resisted, but this would sometimes facilitate things a bit. While he was sitting on the toilet, I also held my hand firmly on his stomach to give him something to press against, which he seemed to find comfort in. It became tiring for the little guy to push so hard, particularly when the stuff he was trying to push out had become dry and compacted (lovely image, I realize).

This whole situation became particularly problematic when Jimmy began school, because as a result of his holding it in (and his body wanting to go), he became a bit gassy and smelly from marks left in his pants, which of course would make him the target of the worst kind of bullying from his peer group. Only at this point could I appeal to his social senses, albeit in the gentlest manner (refer to Chapter 7). I suggested to Jimmy that he would smell like poop if his bottom wasn't cleaned properly, and that his peers would certainly make fun of him if he did. The reason that his bottom might smell like poop, I said, was that it "wanted to come out." He could understand this in the first grade, and I could see that we were starting to make some headway. I was optimistic that I wouldn't have a second grader with the same problem.

Soon thereafter Jimmy began to go into the bathroom himself, but still asked for help cleaning up. Knowing that in school he couldn't get similar help, I reinforced the need for complete cleanup and hand washing there, which he fully acknowledged. Not long thereafter, he began locking the bathroom door and began to refuse help. I made sure there was always a generous supply of wet wipes on the floor next to the toilet and graciously respected his wishes for privacy. Mission accomplished.

Food

Mealtimes can be stressful with the NLD child, but they do not have to be. I cannot stress this point enough. Jimmy has a limited repertoire when it comes to food preferences, but it isn't as limited as it used to be, and it probably isn't as limited as many children who do not have a hypersensitive gag reflex, which he has. He is extremely sensitive to texture of any kind in his mouth, and this has resulted in a strong aversion to many kinds of foods, as I'm sure you can imagine. He has trouble looking at many foods because of this, although I have definitely gotten through to him that it is socially unacceptable to make faces at foods which do not appeal to him for some reason. But he has trouble just looking at certain foods, the textures of which trigger him. At first I became annoyed by this, thinking that he did it for effect, so I planted a bowl of oatmeal (one of his least favorites) on the kitchen counter and spied on him. The look on his face was one of utter revulsion—as if he couldn't imagine how anyone could possibly put something like that in his or her mouth. I discussed this with the people on his team at school, who confirmed that low muscle tone in his mouth could be contributing to this, and suggested implementing some exercises with a bite stick to strengthen same. They explained to me that this could be detected in part by the fact that Jimmy still "chomped" (more developmentally appropriate for a much younger child) rather than rotary chewed (which an older child would do). Still, I don't think there are any exercises on the planet that will get Jimmy to eat oatmeal. The menu of things that Jimmy likes includes:

pizza	American cheese
hot dogs	pasta
bologna	macaroni and cheese
chicken nuggets	green peppers
carrots	bananas

apples	plums
orange juice	pudding
skim milk	chicken
wholewheat bread	cold cereal
pancakes	

The list has gotten a bit longer over the years and, as long as he is growing and is healthy, we don't make a big deal about it. I try not to make food and food-related issues a major focus in the house because as soon as this happens eating becomes a power struggle and you open up a whole can of worms which you really don't want to open. Suffice it to say that, as long as Jimmy is making sensible choices and is eating to nourish his body, I'm not going to harp on broadening the spectrum of those choices. He hits all the food groups; it's just that his variety is a little lacking. The same could be said about me on any given day. During one day of writing this book, for example, I remember Jimmy scolding me for not eating lunch and then having peanut M&Ms® (my favorite food on the planet) in the afternoon.

If he's not talking, he's not learning

I remember very clearly when Dr. Rourke spoke these words to Dave and me when we sat in his office in Windsor, Ontario, back in May of 2001 and discussed NLD and what manifestations to expect in the coming years. One of the most notable differences between a neurologically typical (NT) child and an NLD child that I remember from our discussion with Dr. Rourke during that weekend is that an NT child will learn through discovery, while an NLD child will not (this is discussed in Chapter 1). So, whereas an NT toddler will encounter a rock, pick it up and learn through picking it up that it has weight, texture, taste, smell and possibly impact on little sister's toe (ouch!), the NLD child will stare at the rock and, until such time when the child can ask about it or talk about it, will learn very little about the rock at all.

So, with the NLD child's early command of language skills, he takes full advantage and uses these skills to learn as much as possible about his world through talking, which is essentially taking the place of all other means for him. So, when we are riding in the car and Jimmy is sitting in the back looking out the window, he's running a monologue out loud because that's how he's processing what he sees and therefore digests the different aspects of his world. This is how he learned how far our friends the Peruchs' house was from ours or what color the Currys' house was or where the soccer field was compared to the Martins'. There is no silent learning in the NLD brain. To us, it's a running monologue, a continuum of obvious facts that goes on and on and seems to have no real point, but it's Jimmy's way of making sense out of things and "putting them away" in his brain. A friend of mine, the mother of a child with Asperger's Syndrome, a disorder which presents very much like NLD but is on the autism spectrum, likens her child's brain to his "closet," and tells him that he has to put ideas, fixations, thoughts, etc. on different shelves of the closet until it's the right time to take them out again.

I remember once, before Jimmy was diagnosed, being at a play date with a woman who had a very headstrong little girl. She told me that she was so tired of hearing her child talk that she sat down one day and cried, begging her daughter to be quiet for just five minutes. I never forgot that story and still think about it to this day, maybe because sometimes I wish for quiet. It is difficult at times to listen to endless talking and to not lose patience, particularly after a difficult day when you have three loads of laundry, another child who needs and wants attention and a willing ear, dinner to cook, and countless other things to do that require brain power.

During difficult times, times when Dave and I are both losing patience, or tired of listening, we try to remember Dr. Rourke's advice to think of what the world must seem like to Jimmy. Granted, there are moments when we must remind each other of this concept because there are, after all, no perfect parents. But if you were to ask me if it is difficult to live with a child who talks all the time, I would have to answer that it is probably no more difficult than it is to live with the kind of brain that compels me to talk my way through a day. I can't imagine that I'd like to go to parties either. By the way, my answer would be that I wouldn't trade one single day of living with my son, and I'd mean it.

Organization

Jimmy possesses a multitude of strengths and gifts, but organization is not among them. On any given day, the inside of his desk at school looks like it has been inhabited by a colony of small rodents on speed, complete with dog-eared edges of papers jutting out hither and thither, pencils falling out, books stuffed in so tightly that you can hardly pull them out and, if you do, the whole house of cards comes tumbling out along with them. In Chapter 9, we discussed ways to work with the school, which included different tips to improve organization. Well, his bedroom at home isn't much better. The bed itself resembles the ocean during a hurricane, with covers heaving up and over themselves like the waves in the famous Japanese tsunami painting. The rest of the room is like a crime scene, and you half expect to see yellow police tape sur-rounding the perimeter.

The reason behind teaching organizational skills to the NLD child is to provide him with ways to control his "world," so to speak, by control-ling his immediate surroundings—that is, his work area, his bedroom, etc. If we consider that the NLD child struggles with both temporal (organizing time) and spatial concepts (coordinating physical space), then it really isn't too difficult to see how everyday organization is going to be tough for him. Think about it this way: if there is a mess on a table top, for example, Jimmy will be overwhelmed by the visual stimulation of the mess and have trouble from the get-go figuring out where to start cleaning it up. Once he does, he'll get bogged down in one aspect of the mess and may have difficulty moving toward the "big picture" goal of completing the task. This tendency can be clearly seen when an NLD child is given a multitask direction, for instance. In many instances, the child will take off to obey the two- or three-part direction, only to complete the first portion of the task and then stand, completely dumfounded, having no idea what he is to do next. Alternatively, he may return to you having completed the first portion of the task, quite proud in having done it, never remembering that there was a second or third part of the direction in the first place.

Since Jimmy was very young, I've had him watch me organize his dresser drawers such that his t-shirts are neatly folded in one drawer and his pants are similarly folded in another drawer. When he rummages through the drawers to find something to wear and I find the drawers in disarray, I reprimand him. I don't necessarily punish him by making him refold all of the clothing, but I might ask him to watch me recreate the drawers the way they were before (it would be far too difficult for him to refold all of the clothing, and I know that). By watching me do this over the years, he is fully aware of what those drawers are expected to look like. Now, when I open his drawers to put away laundry, I know when he has rummaged through the clothes and then attempted to refold them and it makes me very proud, no matter how disheveled the attempts are. Further, it is clear to me that Jimmy wants order in his world, because even when there is disorganization around him, he makes consistent attempts to organize certain aspects of his life. For example, every night, after he takes his shower, he lays out the clothes he plans to wear to school the next day. No matter how messy his room is—and by this I mean there can be toys strewn all over the floor, drawings scattered all about and dirty clothes crawling out of the hamper—there will be a neat little pile of clothes at the base of his dresser with a pair of shoes sitting next to it, like soldiers standing on guard.

When it comes to kitchen chores, I have made headway with the same type of tactic as in the bedroom environment. For example, Jimmy knows that after he eats a snack it is not acceptable for him to leave the dishes in the sink, but the first 11 times I told him this (okay, I could be exaggerating) I had to have him watch me take the dishes out of the sink, rinse them off and place them in the dishwasher. On the twelfth time, however, he did this himself, and has done so ever since. Mission accomplished, I'd say. And when he comes down to eat breakfast at our counter/bar area, he really isn't happy until there is an area neatly cleared away. He doesn't want to look at an empty cereal bowl that his dad might have left when he went off to work. Again, these are Jimmy's attempts at ordering his world and taking control of his environment.

Redecorating? Rethink

When I first moved out of Manhattan, I rented an apartment in an old house near the Hudson River. My apartment was directly underneath that of a newly married couple named Jim and Linda, a wonderfully gregarious pair who I found (and still do) to be extremely fun and entertaining. One thing I never forgot is that whenever Linda had trouble sleeping she had the odd habit of rearranging the furniture in their apartment. I guess this calmed her down, tired her out and made her feel productive. I would lay in my bed hearing the scratching and squealing of tables and couches sliding across their floor at all hours of the night. Jim would presumably awaken to a reconfigured apartment the next morning. I think of that from time to time, because such a scene, to an NLD child, would be like one from a horror movie.

There are times when you need to change things, however, to move some toys from the playroom to the storage room; to get rid of old clothes, sell an old car, move some pictures around to make a room seem bigger; rearrange the furniture, for goodness sake. Well, with an NLD child, the fun of doing those things is pretty much history. This is not to say that you cannot change things, as long as you don't mind paying dearly in the form of a miserable child, and I mean a *miserable, miserable child.*

One summer day when my kids were out at camp, I decided to try a different arrangement of the living room furniture. I moved the couch to a different wall and arranged the chairs and a table to enhance the view of the piano. When the kids returned home, my daughter was excited by the change, while Jimmy was deeply disturbed and disconcerted, finding nothing whatsoever refreshing about what I had done. "You've changed way too many things," he said angrily. Even though it was a room he was hardly ever in, I knew that I had shaken his world somehow.

There are ways to get around this, however. These sorts of projects tend to go much more smoothly if you get an initial buy-in from your offspring, and this simply means to somehow involve him in the decision and/or the changing process itself so he can see the transformation taking place. In other words, have them walk in during the movie instead of at the end of it. I have now gotten to the point with Jimmy where I ask him for his opinion on changing things as well as to help me actually move things. It's fun to do together and, as long as he's involved, there are no surprises and no backlash. Much to my surprise (and, at times, chagrin), recently he has taken to rearranging the furniture in his own room, which tells me that either I have turned him on to redecorating or perhaps his sensitivity to change has relaxed just a little bit. Either way, it's pretty funny to see my nine-year-old carrying end tables and lamps up and down the hall to "check out how they would look" in his room.

One, two, Velcro my shoe

During the winter months, as part of the Physical Education (PE) program at Redding Elementary School, the students are provided with cross-country skis and boots and they go out onto the fields behind the school and swish away during the PE period. It's a wonderful activity—great for their cardiovascular health as well as their overall coordination. It is also quite an undertaking for the gym teachers to gather these kids up in their gear and go outside onto the snow without wiping each other out with either skis or poles—or both.

Now, tying shoes is something that nearly every child has mastered by the third grade, but this is an activity that is pretty much a nightmare for the NLD child. However, with the advent of the Velcro shoe and sneaker, there is really no reason at all to have a tie shoe, so the NLD child is given a reprieve from this totally frustrating exercise. But since cross-country ski boots—at least the ones that are available at our school—are the tying type, this proved to be rather problematic for Jimmy. Upon realizing the situation, however, one of the PE teachers did not handle this with the delicacy that she could have, and Jimmy became very ashamed and embarrassed. As a result, I found him hiding behind a door in our laundry room when he arrived home from school one day.

"I had a bad day, mom," he said.

"What happened?" I asked.

"Everyone made fun of me because I can't tie my shoes."

"What do you mean, Jimmy? You don't wear shoes that you have to tie. How would anyone know that?"

"We have to tie our boots in PE for cross-country skiing. I couldn't tie mine, so we couldn't go outside, just because of me. I was taking too long. The teacher said so."

"I'm sure there was another reason why the class didn't go outside."

"It was because of me. Mr. Burger. That's what she said."

I hugged my boy, and told him that I would get it straightened out with the teacher, but that I was sure it was a misunderstanding. I asked Jimmy if he wanted to practice some shoe tying a little later so that maybe the next time it would be easier in PE.

"The teacher said that I'm supposed to practice it at home. I don't want to now."

"Maybe later we can. We don't have to now."

He was extremely upset, and so was I. If, in fact, the teacher really humiliated my son by pointing out that he couldn't tie his ski boots and then exacerbated the situation by blaming him for the fact that the class could not go out to ski, we had a real problem. It was early enough in the day to call the school, so I waited until Jimmy went upstairs to begin his afternoon drawing, and then I called Joan Cone and explained my concern to her. She was equally upset by the story, and we set a team meeting for two mornings later, before the opening of school.

In the meantime, I had the opportunity of talking with Jimmy's classroom teacher, who told me that she was in earshot of the class during the PE period, and actually heard the exchange between the teacher and Jimmy when it was discovered that he could not tie his boots.

Jimmy's account to me, she said, was entirely accurate and exceedingly disturbing to her. She was furious about it and relieved that the situation would be addressed directly. This was shaping up to be an interesting meeting.

Once we were all assembled at the meeting the next morning, everything was handled in a diplomatic if firm manner. As I like to say when I speak at Special Education PTA meetings, life is rarely like the movie *Norma Rae*, where people are standing up on tables and shaking their fists—mostly because you get a lot more funny looks than you do results that way. When we sat around the table and started talking about it, the gym teacher, a normally effusive and quite funny lady, was quite serious and focused on the conversation, and seemed to immediately realize her error. Most importantly, I believe she truly learned something from the information that we gave her about Jimmy in particular and about NLD in general. The system worked: the team assembled and dealt efficiently with a problematic issue which had arisen; the PE teacher learned what not to do next time in a similar case, and agreed to assist Jimmy in the tying of his ski boots as well as to talk to him about what had happened; and this was all accomplished without a single person having to stand on top of a desk or shake a single fist. What a wonderful day.

Family: The support system

When you have a child, you must have a support system. This is a basic fact of life. If you're lucky, you may be able to turn to your extended family for that support system, or you may have a great system of friends and neighbors that help you out from time to time. When you have a child with NLD, it is essential that you take the utmost care in establishing this support system so that you're comfortable that the people caring for your child fully understand his disorder, can communicate with him and make him feel comfortable. What you definitely don't want is to have your child's stress level raised any time he's under someone else's care.

The unfortunate fact of the matter is that just because someone is a member of the NLD child's family doesn't mean that they will necessarily fit this bill. It would be ideal if this was so, but it may not be. As parents, we can go a long way toward facilitating this by providing as much information on NLD as possible to family members. When we received Jimmy's initial diagnosis, I immediately purchased Sue Thompson's (1997) book *The Source for Nonverbal Learning Disorders*, and I made several photocopies of the text. I distributed copies of this to many close family members and discussed as much about NLD as I could. In this way, I felt that they would perhaps better understand what to expect in Jimmy's behavior and would be less apt to misunderstand his actions as rude or disrespectful. They, in turn, found the information very helpful and interesting, and appreciated having something concrete to read about this rather nebulous disorder.

This is not to say that everyone is going to graciously accept all materials you give them and burn the midnight oil studying. There will be folks who interpret all of your attempts to explain your child as psycho-babble, and waste no time at all in telling you, while throwing in such quips as "Aw, he's a perfectly healthy, beautiful boy. He just needs a little firm hand, that's all" or "He's got to apply himself and try a little harder. He needs to eat better food." The point is, you might hear just about everything at one point or another in your journey, but as long as you set your expectations low enough, you'll never be disappointed. Just keep your eye on the goal: when you are trying to set up a system of people to help you take care of your NLD child, whether it be family, friends, neighbors, after-school programs or what have you, do your homework. Make sure that whoever is coming in contact with your child is familiar enough with him and what makes him tick that they will be able to handle the situations which will certainly arise. Otherwise, give them enough information such that they will, or find a better alternative.

Literal speech

The NLD child does not understand the use of implied speech, innuendo, sarcasm, and the like. So, as parents, we must adjust our speech patterns to employ the use of literal speech so as not to confuse our child. This takes some doing. If you stop and think about the way we all tend to speak to one another, I'm sure you can't go for more than a few minutes without using some sort of idiom or figure of speech. These sorts of things really throw the NLD child for a loop. See? I just did it.

The NLD child hears exactly what we say, not what we mean. So we have to be extremely careful that we tell them just what we mean to tell them—no more, no less. You may remember the example I gave earlier in the book about the time I asked Jimmy to "keep an eye on" his little sister. You can well imagine the image that went tearing through his head of having to remove one of his eyes and put it on his kid sister. Some of our figures of speech, when taken literally, can be downright frightening. The literal mind of the NLD child can be a scary place, so we have to break our speech down to its basic parts to remove as much chaos from their world as possible.

Getting it straight

Like most people, I have my own strengths, but a strong memory is not one of them. Jimmy, however, can remember just about everything, and he takes great pride in that. He is like a steel vault of facts, dates and details, and he is never wrong. Whenever we want to recall a family gathering or something that happened on a vacation, etc., we simply call Jimmy and ask him and—boom—we get the answer just like that. As neat as it is to get the information on a dime, it is far more rewarding to see his face fill with pride in being able to answer the question so easily and so consistently.

The NLD child also harbors a keen sense of justice that I find refreshing and unique. Their natural tendency is to tell the truth, even when it is totally incriminating to them. It really doesn't occur to them to lie.

The morning smile

When things are going well, and there is nothing particularly bothering Jimmy, he is one of the easiest children to awaken in the morning. He welcomes me with a heartfelt smile, a warm squeeze, and rises from bed with a minimum amount of prodding. He dresses himself in minutes and bounds downstairs where he prepares his own breakfast. Knowing when it's time to stop eating, he then brushes his teeth and gets his backpack. Mornings with Jimmy are quite simply a joy.

Apologize

One of the most valuable pieces of advice that I can give parents of NLD children is this: don't ever lose the ability to apologize to your child. With this comes the assumption, of course, that we will make mistakes. Of course we will. I would love to say that I have never shouted at my son or used a completely confusing figure of speech at an entirely inappropriate moment, rendering him an emotional mess. But alas, I would be fibbing. When these things happen, as they inevitably do, I immediately go to him, hat in hand, and apologize. He accepts my apology, usually with a pat on my head and a kiss on the forehead, and we go on our merry way, no worse for the wear. I think, by doing this, Jimmy sees that I am indeed flawed, that he isn't the only one in the family that can feel bad about himself at times. It is extremely important to be able to expose this part of yourself to your child—to let him see that the authority figure is capable of culpability, particularly since NLD children have such a keen sense of fairness in the first place. An apology helps clear up any confusion about things. It says "Yes, the rules apply, even to the parents. We made a mistake, and we're sorry." It keeps home safe and secure for them, which is of the utmost importance. To the NLD child, or to any child for that matter, a parent's apology does not show weakness, it shows strength.

Summary

1. One challenge of NLD is living with the almost nonstop chatter that the child will engage in to process the information he is receiving. When times get tough, the best advice is to think of what the world must be like for the child.

2. Teaching organization skills to an NLD child will help him learn how to control his "world" by controlling his immediate surroundings. Give him tips on how to keep his room neat and tidy. Work with him to organize his drawers, set clothes out for the next day, and tidy up his books and toys.

3. Try to avoid redecorating or rearranging furniture without either warning the child or including him in the process.

4. Apprise close relatives of the child's disorder and give them information so that they, too, can learn how to best communicate and interact with the child.

5. Adjust the use of sarcasm, innuendo, and other nonliteral figures of speech. Be accurate, or you will confuse the child. Apologize when you make a mistake.

Chapter 12

Changes in Routine and Moving—A Four-Letter Word

Everything in moderation, even moderation.

Calvin D. Russell

I think we've sufficiently driven home the point that, for the NLD child, routine rules. So it stands to reason that the changes in said routine that accompany such things as family trips, holidays and vacations can really rock the proverbial boat. No, scratch that. If you're not careful, they can come pretty close to sinking the whole darn ship.

The irony here is that these are supposed to be fun activities: the gathering of family, summer vacations, Thanksgiving dinner, and airplane trips to wonderful, exotic, relaxing destinations where time is of no import. It's tough to know where to begin because each of these almost deserves a chapter unto itself. The common denominator is, as you all well know, *novelty*. The NLD kid doesn't like it and reacts badly to it—full stop. Okay, this we all knew from Chapter 1, but it deserves another mention here. There are many more aspects to trips, holidays and vacations than just novelty, and these deserve some attention.

Vacations

Preparation

So you've bought tickets on Tiki Tiki Airlines, packed up your snorkel and the kids' beach toys and you're all taking off on a five-day, all-inclusive funfilled family getaway package where the kids will be enticed with round-the-clock activities and where you and your husband will be able to sit on the beach and drink concoctions out of pineapples while the crystal blue water licks at your toes.

Rewind tape. Before you slather on the SPF 40, make sure you prepare yourself and your NLD child for the kind of trip that this is going to be. In other words, do yourself a favor, and don't expect to surprise this kid with a last-minute question like "Guess what, honey? Tomorrow morning we're all going on a big family adventure" and expect him to be as excited about it as the rest of you.

It is essential, yes, essential, that the NLD child is given plenty of notice about any kind of trip away from home, whether it be for pleasure travel or otherwise. He needs time to prepare himself for this kind of disruption to his life and to his routine before he can even begin to look forward to it. He needs a chance to ask myriad questions about the plane ride: how long will it take to get to the airport, will he have to leave school early, how long will it take to get there, who will drive the plane, etc. Then, there will be questions about the trip itself, about where he will sleep and eat, what types of food there will be, what will the rooms be like, whether or not there will be television, VCR, and other amenities. He'll wonder about missing school, and whether or not he'll be able to make up his homework. As parents, be prepared to address these questions and not be surprised or put off by them.

Once the initial questions are satisfactorily answered, your child will be in the clear to begin looking forward to the trip—and so will you. This is when you should talk to him about setting aside belongings that he would like to bring along. Of course you would only do this for an age-appropriate child—perhaps three years and older. You can designate a corner of his room, for example, where he can set aside small toys, books, favorite shirts, shorts, blankets, etc. This way, he can not only become accustomed to seeing what he will be playing with, wearing etc. each day on the trip, but he can also become increasingly excited about the trip each time he looks at the growing pile.

Accommodations: Hotels vs. condominiums

If you are going to a family resort, condominiums have always seemed to work better for us than hotels. This is because, with Jimmy, having to go to a restaurant for every meal can be very stressful because food choices are often extremely limited. In our experience, for example, Jimmy might want pancakes, but we don't know if that restaurant's pancakes are going to be the kind that he's used to and, when they arrive, Jimmy's anxiety level will be off the charts because, if they aren't, he'll feel guilty on top of hungry on top of frustrated on top of... You get the idea. And then the waitress starts rolling her eyes as if Dave and I should go back to parenting school, and I get the urge to stand on the table and exclaim "You people just don't get it" and, at that moment, I would give my right arm for a box of Bisquick® and a griddle pan to make the pancakes myself.

In addition to the kitchen amenities, condos usually come with VCRs and/or DVD players, which make the transition from home a little easier because your child can bring favorite movies along. This offers the opportunity not only for familiarity and continuity with the home environment, but also periods of "down time" during the vacation days. This is, in my opinion, exceedingly important. When you're on a family vacation, every bit of the daily schedule is essentially turned upside down, from bedtime to getting up time. Meals are different, activities are different, rules are all but abandoned in many cases. The family is trying to do many things together and make the most of its time away so there is, understandably, much more stimulation concentrated in the day than there normally is. Because of this, the NLD child is going to feel overwhelmed and may react to this stimulation in sometimes less than positive ways. If and when this occurs, it's great when the child can go back to the room or condo and sit quietly with a movie or a book and just relax for a while. Many times, this is all it takes to regain some of the calm that he had lost during the chaos of the day. If you can't get a condo, many hotels offer refrigerators and VCRs in the rooms for a per diem fee if you call ahead and make arrangements. It's well worth it.

Bernie, the hotdog guy

Every year, we rent a beach house on the southern New Jersey coast in a town called Sea Isle City. One of the first houses we rented was a blue, slightly run-down duplex on 59th Street, directly on the beach access and right next to the spot where Bernie, a friendly man with a South Philadelphia accent, would set up his shiny silver hotdog stand and feed scads of beachgoers every day under his brightly colored umbrella. Throughout the day you could hear the clanks of the various compartments, sauerkraut, onions, and chili, as his customers made requests to decorate their dogs. Or, on rainy days, the street would be silent and

Bernie would stay home. The 59th Street house was the one that Jimmy loved the most, and he wanted us to rent it the following year. We liked the house well enough, but felt we should try for something a little better, a little nicer. In fact, we did that the next few years, and the kids seemed to have fun each time, although Jimmy did seem to pine for that blue house nestled behind the dunes, probably because it was the first house that he was really aware of vacationing in at Sea Isle, coupled with the fact that he missed being close to Bernie.

Well, last year we decided to rent that same house again, and Jimmy was so excited I thought he might not be able to get through the winter once he heard the news. This time, we shared the house with friends of ours that Jimmy and Shawn know very well who have a 14-year-old son that they dearly love.

I think it was the best week's vacation this family has ever had. Does that mean there weren't any meltdowns? Goodness no. But they were all in an environment of love, support and understanding, No one was stressed, we could all do what we wanted and it was just a great, great time. And there was the ocean, day in and day out. Jimmy and Shawn were in the water more than they were out. We bought ice cream from the Fudgy Wudgy Man. Dave and I swam together for the first time in probably five years. I tried (and failed) to skim board, but the experience offered a great deal of entertainment for many beachgoers. One night, we locked ourselves out of our house, and Dave had to knock on the neighbors' door and climb across their deck to ours in order to get in. We all boogieboarded together, and swallowed lots of sea water. There were no jellyfish. Shawn, with skin as white as a saltine cracker, didn't get sunburn. Our friends' son Kevin talked us into renting a covered, six-person beach surrey (that was about as easy to pedal as a Sherman tank) and we struggled our way up and down the promenade, in stitches practically the whole way. Our friend Darice started a fire in one of the frying pans, but we managed to extinguish it with no human casualties.

We decided to brave the amusements at a nearby park, but the escape proved to be a bit more than Jimmy could handle, and was the first "bust' of the week. We probably should have done a bit of reconnaissance beforehand, but I guess we were on a sort of high from the beginning of the week going so well, and we just went ahead and jumped in. I believe that Jimmy really wanted to enjoy the ride that he chose, but once he actually got on it, his mood changed considerably and quite dramatically. He wanted to get off, and *fast*. I don't have to tell you that carnival personnel aren't exactly trained in customer relations, so his self-esteem wasn't skyrocketing after he left the ride, with his sister crying in tow. We tried to take a break with both of them directly afterward, but it's difficult to find a place for quiet time in an environment of moderately controlled chaos, and Dave and I felt that Jimmy's anxiety level was simply ratcheting up by the minute. We tried to distract him so that Shawn could enjoy some rides, and we were able to do that for a while. He was as good a sport as we could have possibly hoped for him to be, and he went on some rides with his sister and tried like heck to enjoy them. It just wasn't his cup of tea. Luckily, Shawn didn't have a lot of gas in her tank either, so we squeaked out a handful of rides, then soothed whatever savage beasts were left with cotton candy and lemonade and called it a night.

Later in the week, our friend Rocky made his famous Seafood Fra Diablo and we ate it on the back deck in roomy chairs, overlooking the ocean. We strolled into town at night and bought cheesy souvenirs and taffy in the many shops that lined the promenade. Some nights, there was live music on the bandstand about halfway down, and people would be dancing under the silver moonlight. Ours was one of the few weeks of that summer that it didn't rain.

Right next to our house, Bernie the hotdog guy set up his umbrella every single day, and we made lots of visits there, barefoot and sandy. It just doesn't get any better than that. I know this because it's November, and Jimmy and Shawn are still talking about that week in August that we spent in Sea Isle City with our friends the Peruchs. You can bet that we're putting in our reservation request for next year.

Weekends away

If you're going away for a short time and planning to stay at the home of family or friends, for instance, it's best to make sure you have a clear idea of what the sleeping arrangements are going to be ahead of time. If you're comfortable enough to stay in someone's home, I think it's a good idea to discuss the situation of your NLD child with them (if they aren't aware of it already) and be honest about your concerns. If your host has ideas that your child is going to sleep in a big room with "all the kids," for example, and you don't think that's going to work well, then say so. Be diplomatic, but be firm. Something like "That would be really fun, and thank you so much for thinking of it, but I'm afraid it just won't work for

Jimmy" is how I might put it, and then go on to explain why it won't work. Offer to have your child(ren) stay in the room with you and, if this is not an arrangement that can work due to space restrictions, etc., then offer to stay in a hotel.

Our first choice when going out of town to visit family or friends is, in fact, to stay in a hotel, and I am usually very upfront about this. I've gotten to the point in my life where worrying about other people's feelings simply cannot factor into the elaborate equation that must be solved in order to accomplish a weekend away. It comes down to this: we do what works for us, within the parameters we are constrained by, and that's basically it.

This doesn't mean that we run over the top of folks in the process. What we try to do is quite to the contrary in fact. We make it our business to stay out of everyone's way, to try to occupy our own space, establish our own oasis, if you will, for the duration of the visit. As we emphasized in our discussion of the family vacation earlier, it is very important for the NLD child to have a place to go, particularly during the hectic daily schedule of vacationing, where he can have quiet, down time. It's the same for a weekend away. Think about it: even if you explain yourself silly, wouldn't it be kind of awkward for your child to walk into your friend's house after a day out and shut himself in a room, asking everyone to leave him alone? Even the most understanding of friends or family members might find this a bit offputting, and it might just add a touch of stress to the evening's festivities. Better to have a little break for yourselves, a chance to rest and freshen up at your respective "places' and then reconvene at your friends' house later on.

In the unfortunate instance that someone gets offended that you chose this route rather than to accept their hospitality, they usually understand once you explain the limitations you're operating under. If not, then I say tough darts. And remember: this isn't just about the comfort of your NLD child. It's about the dynamic of your family as a whole. When the NLD child is under a lot of stress and anxiety, everyone is uncomfortable and the whole equilibrium of things is completely thrown off. I know that when Jimmy is out of sorts, Shawn is thoroughly ill at ease, and it isn't until things are running smoothly again that she feels better. When the kids are in a funk, Dave and I are, well, cranky. I don't think a family weekend away is the time for this type of dynamic to be happening. If you know what to do to make it work, then do it. Don't worry about everyone else, because they'll usually understand that you're doing what's best for your family. And even if they don't, you'll have to take comfort in knowing that you're doing the right thing.

Holidays—Oh joy, oh boy, oh help

I saw a movie several years ago starring Holly Hunter and Ann Bancroft entitled *Home for the Holidays*. The story followed a dysfunctional family as it reunited during the Thanksgiving holiday. At one point during this funny but sad journey, Holly Hunter's character muttered to herself, "It'll all be okay if we just stuff ourselves."

Whether it be Christmas, Chanukah, Thanksgiving, Easter, Groundhog Day, Passover, July 4, whatever you choose, if there is an occasion involving the gathering of large amounts of people where there is the potential for some relation by blood, in my estimation you're running the risk of possible meltdown either for yourself or for your NLD child. Okay, maybe that's a little overdramatic, but at least I got your attention. Now let's back up and approach this discussion in a different way. I'm going to use Christmas as an example here because I've gone through so many of them. You can fill in the blank with any holiday you choose.

Let me review the high points. As we touched on briefly in Chapter 6 (Socialization), many holiday gatherings mark meetings with family folk which your child might not have laid eyes on for the better part of a year and therefore is largely, if not entirely, uncomfortable with. Even for the neurologically typical child, this is like being thrown into the deep end of a cold pool. But for the NLD child, this is tantamount to being tossed off a cliff into a dark fog. Add to the mix that the child is expected to not only talk to these family members who feel like total strangers, but to let them make physical contact with him, hug and kiss him, perhaps touch his head, his face, invade his personal space, his "bubble," while he remains calm, even returns the affection. Are we kidding ourselves? When we look at it this way, of course the idea seems preposterous, but this is in effect what we ask our child to do when we thrust them into the thick of holiday gatherings. Just because these are family affairs, it doesn't mean that the NLD child will assimilate any better than he would to any other large gathering of people. To him, the faces are strange, the noises are confusing and the food is weird. The child is probably already wiped out by the weeks of festivities that have led up to the holiday: the school parties, the community festivities, the out-of-the-ordinary household activities that normally accompany a holiday, so he's coming into the gathering with a handicap. Add it all up and what have you got? You've got a simple, no-bake recipe for a meltdown. To avoid this kind of a scenario, I'd like to share a few tips for approaching the holidays with an NLD child.

Think horses, not zebras

Try to keep things as simple as possible—and, believe me, I know this can be a tall order, especially around the major holidays. I'll go back to the example of Christmas because this covers so much ground. It's difficult to insulate your NLD child from the inevitable overstimulation that occurs when you're walking through the mall or the toy store, but you can certainly control the climate within the walls of your home.

Traditions

I make it a point to establish meaningful and peaceful traditions around the holidays that will be fun for the whole family, will bring them together, and will serve to de-stress everyone (especially Jimmy). These can be conventional types of traditions such as baking cookies or decorating the tree, which have become real favorites in my house. Jimmy and Shawn look very much forward to spending long, cold afternoons with me and my Kitchen Aid®, watching the different doughs take form in the large, spinning silver bowl and helping me add ingredients. They particularly love the cookie press for the Spritz butter cookies, and adding food coloring to the dough to make red and green wreath or Christmas tree cookies.

Another favorite tradition of ours is decorating the Christmas tree. I'd love to tell you that we tromp to the community tree farm in our winter boots, ax in hand, and choose a tree to cut down, then whack it off at the base and haul it to our four-wheel drive and roll it home to a blazing fire in the wood stove, hot chocolate and an afternoon of stringing popcorn and singing carols. But we don't. I go up in the attic and blow the dust off the same artificial tree Dave and I bought when we first got married. I drag it down the stairs in two pieces, and put it together in the living room, then spend about a half hour trying to make it look like a tree by pushing the bows back away from the center of the tree and spreading out the branches. Then I spritz my Crabtree and

Evelyn® pine scent spray around the living room and the tree really comes alive. The kids get excited because they know that pretty soon we'll be ready to string the lights and put the star on the top. Then it'll be time to dig into the box of ornaments and the fun will really start.

This offers an opportunity for us to relax together and look through the equivalent of a lifetime of memories for me. Some of the Christmas tree ornaments in that cardboard box I have had since I was a little girl myself, and I can share many stories with Jimmy and Shawn as we hang them on those annoying little wire hangers that are incessantly tangled around each other. Surprisingly, my children seem to enjoy these stories and even ask questions as if they want to know more. I think they enjoy my reverie and the fact that they have my undivided attention for that period of time. They are also proud of the fact, knowing how much I value those ornaments, that I allow them to handle them and hang them on the tree so freely.

There are memories resurfaced, memories shared, and memories created, all in the same afternoon. It's one of our favorite activities of the season and, when we're done, there's such a fine feeling of both satisfaction and anticipation. We've created a beautiful display, and Santa is coming to see it.

Take a break

As important as it is to establish traditions and to do things with your children (and the NLD child is certainly no exception to this rule, and may, in fact, need a bit more attention) I believe that it is equally important to do nothing with your children—at least sometimes. Whatever you call it—vegetate, hang, waste time, take up space, contemplate your collective navels, listen to the grass grow, waste your batteries, whatever. Sit on the couch and listen to music, or get up and dance to it (we do this quite often and it's great for blowing off steam), read a book together, or take turns guessing what the dog is thinking. You get the idea. You'd be surprised at some of the wonderful impromptu discussions that will arise during these times, discussions you might not otherwise have the opportunity to enjoy.

The craziness which befalls the holiday season can reduce the most neurologically typical of us to a melted down mess, so it only stands to reason that it can be a time of stress and anxiety for the NLD child. Common sense would tell you, the parent, to keep an eagle eye and a tight fist on routine, and try to maintain a sense of normalcy when and where you can. There are wonderful joys in the special occasions that are holidays. There are also extrinsically imposed stresses that simply don't need to be allowed into the home. You be the judge of which is which, and stand firm. Let your instinct be your guide.

Show, don't tell

This is the first lesson that we writers must learn, and it always makes the difference between good and bad writing. You show what's happening in a scene with your characters and dialogue rather than tell what's going to happen with cumbersome adjectives and adverbs. It's the same with parenting, believe it or not. You can tell your children what's right all day long, but until you show them what's right, they're not really going to believe you.

I think the idea of "Show, Don't Tell" is relevant here because, particularly during the holidays, there are many neighborhood and school organized efforts to gather dinners, gifts, clothing, etc. for the less fortunate families in our communities. While this is a wonderful practice which I support and encourage my children to not only understand but to also participate in, I also feel it is important to continue such practices throughout the year. For any child, but perhaps particularly for the NLD child (who tends to fixate on what is happening within his own "universe"), such revelations are valuable in that they provide much needed insights into the "real" world. As a parent, I find it very rewarding to see the sort of catharsis on their faces when it finally registers that we are packing bags with things like flour, sugar, salt and paper towels because people may not have the wherewithal to purchase these things for themselves. Either Jimmy or Shawn may say "Wow, I guess we're pretty lucky that we have enough." It really doesn't matter who comes to this realization first, because one will hear it from the other. If they both arrive at it simultaneously, glory be, I say. Either way, we are indeed lucky, because this family ended the day with a great appreciation for something that they may not have had when they woke up in the morning. Appreciating what you've got, and embracing it—now that's a lesson that's never lost, and I don't think it's too far a leap for parents of special needs children to see the meaning in that.

Moving—A four-letter word

Imagine if you will, the most difficult set of circumstances you possibly can for the typical NLD child. Give up? Okay, let me help you out. How about this for starters:

- change houses

- change towns

- change schools

- change church

- change...*EVERYTHING*.

Okay, so maybe it sounds a little dramatic, but this is essentially what happened in Jimmy's eyes when we sold our house and moved from Newtown to Redding, Connecticut, in the winter of 2001. Of course, he was not aware that the primary reason we were making this gargantuan move was because we felt that the private Montessori school he was attending in Newtown did not offer an appropriate environment for him; nor did the public school system (I have close friends who went to mediation with the school system because of services that they believed should have been provided for their son—this may have shaded my view somewhat). Dave and I began to research all of the different educational options available to us, including private schools in the area such as Eagle Hill in Greenwich and Southport. The problem with these schools was that Jimmy would be in a small size classroom with only learning disabled children, which would not help him mainstream socially. This was of great concern to both Dave and me, not to mention the upwards of $37,000 per year price tag that went along with this option.

We then remembered that when we attended a seminar on NLD about a year or so before in Meriden, CT, we canvassed one of the rooms and asked if there were any teachers there. To our utter surprise, there were almost none, except at one table there was a group of three people from the Redding/Easton school system. That stuck in our minds so much so that, when we were looking at towns and school systems to consider, I decided to call the Redding and Easton School Systems and talk with them about what they had to offer in the way of Special Services. I called Redding first, and set up an appointment with the director of special education for the following week.

Dave and I attended that meeting together, walking in with a list of questions that looked like a receipt from a pre-Thanksgiving grocery store spree. But as soon as we saw *The Source for Nonverbal Learning Disorders* by Sue Thompson on the director's desk, we knew we were dealing with someone who understood the lay of the land (or at least wanted us to think she did). Our subsequent discussion with her confirmed as much, and it was a great comfort, especially after coming from a school where I had to write my own IEP for Jimmy. After our 30-minute meeting with Mary Lou Torre of Special Services at Redding Elementary School, Dave and I left the building, faced each other and said, "This is the place for Jimmy." There is no better feeling in the world than knowing you've found the right school for your NLD child.

We thought the hard part was over. Boy, were we wrong. Deciding to move was only the first in a long series of steps of actually relocating our family. It was an entirely different story to actually convince Jimmy that this was the best thing to do. We couldn't possibly tell him that we were going to leave Newtown because we didn't think it was a good place for him—the responsibility would be far too much for him to bear—so we gradually started to tell him that we had to leave because of a change in Dad's job, which wasn't entirely untrue. Dave's job was coincidentally moving to Stamford, and the commute from Redding would be decidedly better for him.

At first, any talk of selling our house to strangers was met with utter disdain, to say the least. Even worse was the idea that we would (a) buy a house that was currently owned and lived in by another family and (b) actually move all of our belongings into it after they moved theirs out. What an awful notion, according to Jimmy. Who would come up with such a barbaric idea, anyway? Needless to say, this was not a pleasant period in our home, and we found ourselves embroiled in countless debates with our son in an effort to allay some of his fears, but to no avail. He was tied in knots, and had convinced himself that he was staying in Newtown, and that was it. We could all move if we wanted to, but he wasn't going anywhere.

Things only got a little more bearable when Dave and I actually found a house that we wanted to buy and took both Jimmy and Shawn to see it. It wasn't that the house was necessarily better or worse, but it provided something concrete for Jimmy to focus on which made the whole thing real to him. It was a bonus that he found some things in the house that he liked, even though he resisted the notion with every molecule of his body.

As moving day approached, we tried to keep things as normal as possible (no easy task when there are boxes everywhere, brown paper lining the floors and strangers walking through the house sticking small orange labels on the furniture). We explained to Jimmy what was going to happen ahead of time so that he would understand the chronology of things and wouldn't be afraid, for example, that our belongings were going out the door and never coming back. He was aware that the moving company employees would load things on their trucks and hold them for the night before we moved into the new house and then bring them there and unload them again. He repeated this back to us several times, which told us he needed the comfort of that information.

Once we moved into the new house, I made it my business to unpack everything as quickly as possible—particularly the children's rooms and the play room area—so that they would have familiar, comfortable spaces to live in. I knew this meant a lot to their immediate ability to settle in. Once that was done, I hunkered down to the rest of the house, and I would say that within a week's time I had the bulk of it looking pretty unpacked and settled. Friends that came over were amazed at how the house looked, that I even had pictures on the walls after a week. But it was very important to me to have the house looking like a home, and not like a place littered with moving blankets and cardboard boxes. This would only have added to the feeling of displacement that Jimmy was already suffering.

The actual logistics of the relocation were a bit rocky, but fairly shortlived compared to the emotional upheaval of the move. Once we were physically settled in, we had to deal with the issue of transitioning Jimmy into the new public school, which would certainly be a horse of a different color. I was still commuting both kids to the Montessori school in Newtown, which I would do for the remainder of the academic year. I had paid the tuition through the end of the year, and any further disruption to Jimmy's life would be completely counterproductive. We'd finish out the next few months at Montessori, and Jimmy and Shawn would begin at Redding Elementary School in September.

Over the summer, I enrolled the children in the local park and recreation camp program for a few weeks to try to assimilate them to the school environment (the camp took place on school grounds) and to familiarize them with the faces that they would be seeing come the fall.

They seemed to enjoy the program for the most part, and even made a few friends. Over the summer, Jimmy also did some testing with the school psychologist and, since this was a person that he took quite a liking to, this helped him become more comfortable with the idea of attending the school in the fall.

Still, as September neared, I could sense the increase in anxiety that Jimmy was feeling. But there was also a little excitement in the air with the idea of taking the bus to school (instead of having me drive him, as was the case with the Montessori school). Also, he seemed to hit it off with his new teacher, Ms. DeBonis, at the classroom visit the week or so before school started. This helped ease his anxiety somewhat. All things considered, Jimmy was pretty ready for the start of school.

The first day seemed to go off without too much of a problem. That is, if you don't count Jimmy's getting on the wrong bus at dismissal time (he didn't get nearly as freaked out as I did, which is the good news—and thank God for cell phones, which every bus driver has). But as the weeks progressed, Jimmy's anxiety level increased as bullying and various social issues crept up on him. There were many days and weeks when Jimmy would exit the bus and hurl his backpack to the ground, without saying a single word to me, and stomp into the house. He hated the school, the kids, the bus driver, the house, the town, everything, and that was it.

Those weren't fun days, but we managed to work it out with the help of communication with each other, with the teacher, and with the educational team. Most of the issues centered around Jimmy having to adapt to a new environment and the kids in his class learning to accept him and his differences. Eventually, with the help of a great teacher and a lot of perseverance by everyone (including Jimmy), a turnaround happened. Again, we're not talking a Disney movie here. It's all very gradual, and you take your little victories where and when they come. But they come if you're patient and you stick with it, and with an NLD child, that's exactly what you learn to do.

Jimmy still has a lot of tough days, as do we all. Now, 18 months later, he has gotten to the point where he can tell off a classmate when they're saying something to him that's totally inappropriate and bullying. He can also say something funny and get the whole class laughing. He's learned, I believe, to embrace his differences much better than he could a year ago.

Moving suggestions

If moving is something that you must face as a family, here are some suggestions that may help you on your journey. If, like we did, you decide to make a move based in large part on the educational needs of your NLD child, I believe it would be a disservice to place this burden on him. I'm not, of course, suggesting that you lie to your child, but I am advising you to be conscious of what kind of responsibility he can handle.

If you do have to sell your house, avoid having your NLD child in the home during showings. You can well imagine that if these children have difficulty when guests attend a party in their home, there's going to be plenty of upset when strangers come to size things up for a possible purchase.

Do most of your early house hunting research without your children. It's tiring for adults—just think of what it must do to kids. You especially don't want to involve the NLD child in the process until you've nearly made up your mind on a location and a house.

On moving day, chances are you'll have the kids at home with you. Take the time to introduce the movers to them so that the children will be familiar with the folks (usually rather large men) that will be tromping through their house and taking their belongings out. Explain to the movers ahead of time that there is some pretty hefty anxiety about the whole situation, particularly with respect to the NLD child and his things, and ask that some special care be taken when emptying his room, for example. On our moving day from Newtown, Jimmy ended up having quite a good time with the moving crew, particularly when they brought fresh pastries on the second day and let him toss a few things to them out of the second-floor window.

Inevitably, the NLD child is going to have to leave the old house, and this is not an easy thing for him to do. Since you will probably have to either stay with friends, family or in a hotel for a night or two, it is essential that the child has his own care package to take along which contains:

- a favorite stuffed animal or toy
- familiar blanket
- activities/games
- favorite pajamas
- familiar foods

- books

- photos of old home/neighbors

- change of clothes.

Once the family has moved into the new house, the comfort level of the NLD child will become a function of how quickly the small city of brown boxes around him disappears. This is not too difficult to understand when looking at it from the perspective of how these children's minds work. Additional chaos in the form of mountains of boxes, piles of belongings hither and thither—this will only serve to exacerbate an already turbulent situation. In short, try to organize the new digs in a hurry. Make it look like home, even if making it look that way stresses you out. Believe me, you're doing it for the right reason.

Okay, I know that bribery is definitely not at the top of the list of Great Parenting Tips, but offering your child(ren) an incentive so that they look forward to moving into their new home isn't such a horrible idea, is it? In our case, I told the kids that we would get a dog (yes, I've been known to jump into the deep end of the pool). This was pretty remarkable a gesture given that I swore I would never, and I mean never ever, have anything of the canine variety. Too dirty, too smelly, too apt to sniff where they shouldn't, too hairy, I said. In fact, I always sneered at the mere idea of it, being a resolute cat person since childhood. Enter Maddy, our adopted yellow Lab/Husky mix, now three years old and a bona fide member of the family. A word to the wise: for those of you with an aversion to vacuuming, goldfish aren't a bad place to start in the negotiating process.

Throughout the entire moving process, it is very important to continually reassure your NLD child (and all of your children) that, while you may be changing the house that you live in, your *home* is wherever your family is, and this never changes as long as you are all together. I told this to my children quite often during our moving journey, and it seemed to bring them comfort and security. It didn't hurt Dave and me to hear it either.

Life gets messy

Two months before this book was to be delivered to the publisher, my father was diagnosed with a malignant and aggressive form of brain cancer. His life, and that of all of my family, was immediately turned upside down as we began trips to the hospital for my dad's various testing, spending time by his side while he underwent cranial surgery and then recuperated from same, taking care of my mother, who has her own health problems, and all the various struggles that come with this terrible ordeal. Needless to say, the environment within our home has been riddled with upset and disruption. Dave frequently left work early to get the kids off the bus, beds were not made, laundry was left undone, dishes were in the sink instead of in the dishwasher or washed and in the drainer. The kids might see me crying at my desk or on the phone, and I was not very talkative. But Jimmy, a child who isn't supposed to be able to deal with any of this very well at all, was a great comfort to me. When he asked me what was wrong, I told him that his grandpa was very sick. He then asked me, straight out, "Mom, is he going to get better?"

I told him the truth. "I don't know, Jimmy."

To that, he replied straight from the heart. "Well, I hope he does, because I really love talking to him."

"Me too, honey."

Summary

1. Give the NLD child as much notice as possible about a trip away from home. Make sure sleeping arrangements and schedule are determined beforehand, and communicate those to the child. Pack familiar things to reduce novelty. For vacations, opt for a condo rather than a hotel room, to enable relaxing down time in the event of sensory overload.

2. Holidays can be stressful for everyone, but particularly the NLD child. Try and keep some regular traditions and as much routine as possible. During times of over-stimulation, make room in the schedule for decompression time and quiet.

3. Moving is probably the biggest type of upheaval. It can involve the change of home environment, routine, school and many other familiar aspects of the child's world. Helping the child adapt to the new environment is critical to his successful transition. Recruit the help of family, friends, teachers and everyone else the child comes in contact with.

Chapter 13

Getting Involved

Tell me and I'll forget; show me and I may remember; involve me and I'll understand.

Chinese Proverb

I used to be one of those parents who would readily shy away from getting involved in any kind of school or church activity. I think I viewed it as some kind of conspiracy by society to invade my privacy, to "suck" me into a chasm of unsolicited familiarity, to ravage me in some way, to recruit me as one of "those" mothers—you know, the PTA, the "room mother" types, the kind that became fixtures at all the school functions, games, events, etc. I honestly don't know where this fear came from. I must have been traumatized at a very young age by some horrific extracurricular activity or held hostage by a den full of hot glue-gun bearing women. All I know is that if, ten years ago, you told me that I would now be President of a Special Education PTA in Redding, Connecticut, I would have told you that you'd lost your mind.

Well, the moral of this story is: never say never, and never say always. And, above all, don't ever try to take away my hot glue gun. It has gotten me out of more than a few binds.

Parent support groups

There was a time when the phrase "support group" conjured images in my head of a group of women sitting in a circle drinking herbal tea and complaining to each other about how awful everything in their lives had become or, worse, gazing at themselves in hand held mirrors chanting "I am okay, and people can like me." Well, I know now that this is not an accurate notion, that there is a lot to be gained from sharing one's thoughts and struggles with others in similar circumstances. This is not to say there are not poorly run support groups around, because I know for a fact that there are. In fact, I have attended some that felt more of the "whiny" variety, and I simply bowed out of them and either (a) found another group which I felt was more productive in terms of individuals sharing thoughts and ideas in positive and helpful ways; or (b) started my own group.

A parent support group can run the gamut from the informal gathering of a group at someone's house to more regularly scheduled meetings of an organization with a more formal charter. However, it doesn't have to be anything fancy and, in my experience, the simpler the better. Sometimes, a group of parents gathering at someone's home on a rotating basis, perhaps once a month, is a great start. An organic beginning might be that two parents meet each other because their children were introduced at school. I met another parent through our children becoming friends at school. Consider the story of Jimmy and Jack.

Jimmy and Jack

Jimmy was still pretty new in the elementary school when Jack's parents went to visit the head of Special Services there and told them that they would be moving into town during the summer and would be enrolling Jack, who had been diagnosed with Asperger's Syndrome, in the fourth grade for the coming fall. After talking to them and, subsequently, meeting Jack, the people in Special Services knew that Jimmy and Jack had a lot in common and that Jimmy would probably be able to help make Jack's transition into the new school a bit easier. So, they developed a kind of "buddy" plan where Jack would come to visit the school once a week for the last few months of the third grade year, and spend a little time in Jimmy's classroom. Jimmy could show him the ropes, give him an idea about what goes on in the classroom, and get him a little used to life at the elementary school. Also, Jack could get used to some of the faces he was going to be seeing in the fall.

By the end of the school year, Jack had a basic lay of the land as far as the elementary school was concerned, and Jimmy felt less like the new kid on the block and more like a mentor, like he had really helped someone else out. It was a good formula all the way around. The school told us that the parents were good people, and that they might want to contact us to try to get the boys together over the summer. I was more than enthusiastic about the idea, doing everything short of sending up fireworks to get them to encourage a phone call from Jack's family to ours. But I heard nothing over the summer, and Jimmy told me that he didn't see Jack in any of the summer camp sessions that he was in.

Once the new school year began, Jack turned up in Jimmy's class, and my son continued to take the newcomer under his wing. Theirs was a slow friendship to grow. Jimmy was still trying to find his way in this complex maze of social relationships, and he wasn't quite sure where Jack fit into that maze. He felt, somehow, that Jack had been handpicked for him by the grownups in his life to be his friend, and he was resisting it. I, of course, assured him that we just wanted him to help Jack out any way he could, but that he was free to choose any friends he wanted.

During the first few weeks of the school year, I received a call from Joan Cone, who told me that Jack's parents had expressed an interest in having Jimmy come over to their house because Jack had been talking about him at home. They had wondered if they could call me, but didn't want to overstep. Joan wondered if she could give them my phone number. I said that perhaps it would help if I was to call them directly, and just take all of the anxiety out of the process. She really liked the idea, and gave me their name and number.

There is nothing quite as comforting or as immediately familiar as speaking with another mother of an LD child. When I called Jack's mother, there seemed to be no need for the normal niceties. We just got into it—the discussions about perseverations, the struggles, the daily "stuff" that we go through, and what a relief it was to be able to speak freely about it and to have a friend for our child at school and, even better, another home where we knew he could go and be comfortable. We wouldn't have to worry that the mom wouldn't "get it" or would freak out if he started to talk nonstop about her microwave or the inner workings of their television set.

We arranged a play date for Jimmy and Jack, and it has been the first of many. Theirs has grown into a steadfast and strong friendship.

Special Education PTA (SEPTA)

SEPTA is a Special Education Parent Teacher Association, so it is a PTA that works as part of the regular PTA, but focuses on the special education population of the school community. SEPTAs can be extremely valuable and effective organizations that can provide a much needed "bridge" between the teacher and the parent, a link which is so vital particularly where special education is concerned. The goals of SEPTA are as follows:

1.   To support and educate parents as to their children's right to a free and appropriate education which is designed to meet their unique learning styles.

2.   To educate the community as to the realities of special education.

3.   To work to establish community programs to benefit resident families.

Since parents are the most important advocates for their children's education, SEPTAs provide many opportunities for them to learn how to best fulfill this important role. In addition, they offer valuable networking opportunities with other parents of special needs children, which can prove not only very helpful by way of support but also very practical when trying to locate referrals for doctors, therapists and other professionals.

When we moved to Redding, I wasn't aware of what a SEPTA was, much less whether or not one existed in this town. In Newtown, the town I had moved from, I had attended a few meetings of a parent support group for children with special needs, and while I found the parents there had many good ideas and insights, I also found that there wasn't a lot of organization or purpose in the group. In other words, there were weeks when we would end up listening to one member drone on and on about a particular struggle she was having with her child and the school, or about a complaint she had with a particular teacher or administrator. Now, I'm not necessarily saying there isn't a place for this type of "sounding board" situation. Certainly, parents of special needs children—all of us, for that matter—need to have channels for our gripes. But as a parent of a child with NLD, I was looking for a group where I could go to gather information and ideas and find positive reinforcement for myself and for my child. I didn't want to wallow in the negativity of others. It reminded me of the oh so beautiful review given to me by a dear Australian friend after he went to see the movie *Titanic*.

He said, "Crikey, if I want to go watch people drown for three hours, I'll just go to work."

The point here is: it's fine to get together with friends or other parents and whine, if that's what you want or need to do. But when you're ready to organize and get something done, then maybe you're ready to form or join a SEPTA. Once I moved to Redding, got myself and my family settled, and got Jimmy more or less acclimated into the school, I started to know different parents in the school and I learned that there was a small SEPTA in the process of being formed by a woman named Susan, so I gave her a call.

My first conversation with Susan told me that she was really a one-woman show and, further, that she definitely needed some help. Susan was a single mom with two children, and both children had a considerable degree of special needs. Her experience with the school system had not been the most positive, so she was coming at the whole effort with more of a negative bias than I was, but I felt that we sort of leveled each other out to a certain degree. She probably had more experience than I did, I told myself. I'm the newcomer, and she's the sage veteran. I'll learn from her, and perhaps I'll bring a fresh perspective. The important thing is that the SEPTA comes to fruition.

Susan told me that there would be an initial meeting in a few weeks and that she expected at least a dozen or so people to show up. I assured her that I would be there to help. The night of the first meeting came and I made sure to arrive on time. I was happy to finally meet Susan face to face as well as a representative from the Connecticut PTA by the name of Kevin Daly (who was subsequently elected President of the Connecticut PTA). Kevin drove down all the way from Meriden to attend the meeting, and was entirely enthusiastic about Susan's idea to start the SEPTA. He had brought several different handouts which he arranged on a table for the attendees to take home, and told us that he would give a talk about the advantage of having SEPTA work in alliance with the regular PTA. He added that he would always be available to attend meetings or to answer any questions we might have. Kevin was a wealth of information, and I was quite impressed with his level of commitment to the whole process. During the course of the night, I found out that he too had a son with special needs who was now attending high school in Meriden, and that Kevin also worked as a child advocate.

The meeting was very poorly attended, but we still managed to get some business accomplished. By the end of the meeting, I had been nominated by Susan to be Secretary of the new SEPTA, and I was excited at the prospect of this new mission. Over the next several months, Susan and I put our noses to the grindstone and drummed up nearly 25 new members, attended some meetings and brainstormed with SEPTAs in neighboring towns, got ideas for fundraising, and even ran an event or two on our own school premises. We opened a bank account, elected officers, got insurance, wrote by-laws, the works.

During this school year, I am working very closely with the Director of Special Services, who has created a Parent Information Committee to encourage the exchange of information between parents and teachers/administrative personnel. I am a member of this committee along with Jack's dad who has earned a doctorate in parenting. We have become friends and hope to be able to work together to get some positive things done both with the committee and with the SEPTA. In addition, the Special Services Department is increasing in-service training of the staff in the area of nonverbal learning disorder, an area in which they felt the level of experience was lacking.

The bottom line is: If you're a parent of a special needs child, it helps to get involved in the process of your child's educational experience. Even if you hire an advocate, you have to be on top of what's going on. Be one step ahead of the game. There's no other way to understand what's happening on a day-to-day basis. There just isn't.

Seminars, workshops, conferences, etc.

By joining any number of associations and organizations, many of which are listed in the Resources section at the end of the book, you will become aware of many different seminars, workshops, conferences and the like which are scheduled all over the country at various times throughout the year. I have found these to be very enlightening, particularly during the early years of Jimmy's diagnosis when Dave and I were at the low end of the NLD learning curve. At this stage of the game, we go to focus on more specific workshops for specific age group categories as well as for networking opportunities—to speak with other parents and professionals, etc. But many of the conferences have different options that you can consider such as half day, etc.

There are also many lectures and small workshops that are given in local libraries, for example, that offer much needed information on how to advocate for your child in a PPT meeting, or how to interpret the new

IEP forms. These are very valuable for parents because they take the mystery out of reading these rather complicated forms and they provide a comfortable forum to ask questions and to talk with other parents who face similar challenges. These types of lectures are usually run by either child advocates or educational consultants—in either case, these are professionals whose numbers you might want to have handy in your PDA for use on a later date.

Read, read, read

In the Bibliography you'll find a list of books that I have found exceedingly useful throughout my personal journey as the parent of a child with NLD. I would encourage you to refer to them for information as well as inspiration, as I have done.

It is also vital, I believe, as a parent of a special needs child, to keep abreast of any changes in legislation regarding Special Education Law, any new ideas and insights from policymakers, as well as research findings regarding therapies, treatments and/or educational programs for special needs children that may be underway in different areas of the country. Two websites that I have found particularly interesting for this type of information are: *www.schwablearning.org* and *www.wrightslaw.com*. Both of these sites are very user friendly, have numerous links to different articles and useful information that the user can print for future reference as well as anecdotal stories that I have found to be inspirational and helpful. On the Schwab site, there is the added benefit of something called Spark Top.org™, which offers peer support to LD kids through a message board where they can find helpful hints and also talk to each other about homework problems and other topics, so they don't feel alone.

Pay attention

I remember, as a young girl growing up in Wappingers Falls, New York, listening to a neighbor of ours become outraged after attending meetings of our local school board. She would amble across the street and stand in our driveway, ranting to my father about this or that injustice and how it would inflate our taxes or negatively impact the education of the children, and what a travesty it all was. My dad would listen patiently as he watered the lawn or weeded or whatever he was doing, adding his two cents whenever he could. I would ask him later what she was on about, and he would diplomatically submit that she was a very intelligent woman who took a great interest in what was happening in the town. I could never really understand why anyone would attend those sorts of meetings, and this sentiment of mine continued up until the past couple of years. Now I'm one of those people—just as avid, just as ranting. And, mind you, there aren't many of us that attend consistently. In my town, I'd say there are about six or seven women that attend just about every school board meeting. I like to call the group the Seven Wonders of My World because, on those nights of school board meetings—which sometimes run for over four hours—it's such a great comfort to walk into that auditorium after a long day of life and see those same, steadfast faces, often worn out, but still present, pads in hand and glad to see me, every single time. It's a group that will continue its dedication and that is willing to put in the time necessary because it affects all of us and all of our children in so many ways. It gives us all a great sense of community, of belonging. Particularly for me, as the parent of a special needs child, it keeps me from feeling so alone in my journey.

That's why it's so important to keep yourself involved and informed. You'll find that there are many avenues to find information, yes, but you'll also find just as many channels of support and camaraderie. To do this, however, you have to take the first step, and that involves making yourself known as a person who is willing to get things done, to make a difference. It takes some work, but the rewards are countless. So, whether or not your child has a learning difference, I would encourage you to attend the local school board meetings and brush up on the issues. Chances are, if you're reading this book, there is no reason on earth why you shouldn't be attending, because everything that is happening there is of paramount importance to you and to your child. Believe me.

Summary

1.   Getting involved with the various support groups and parent/teacher organizations helps the parent of a special needs child learn, get involved in the child's education process, and feel less isolated on the journey.

2. Parent support groups can range from informal gatherings at someone's home to regularly scheduled meetings of an organization with a more formal charter. They help parents share thoughts, ideas and information, and also form the basis for some lasting, meaningful friendships.

3. A SEPTA is a Special Education Parent Teacher Association, a smaller, more specialized organization within the regular PTA which focuses on the needs of the special education population of the school community. These are valuable and effective organizations that provide a much needed bridge between teacher and parent.

4. The goals of SEPTA are to support and educate parents as to their children's education rights, to educate the community regarding special education, and to establish programs in the schools and community to benefit families.

5. There are many seminars, workshops and other meetings scheduled all around the country in a given year. This is an efficient and effective way to get up the learning curve on LDs or even to find out about new, cutting edge research and services.

Chapter 14
Seeking Outside Help for Your NLD Child

The happiness of a man in this life does not consist in the absence but in the mastery of his passions.

Alfred Lord Tennyson

As important as it is for the NLD child to receive the appropriate accommodations and modifications to his school curriculum and environment, it is equally important for you as parent to make sure that your child is receiving whatever help he needs outside of the classroom. Since many of the deficits inherent in NLD manifest themselves socially, you may find (as I have) that seeking the services of a therapist outside the school is a good idea. In the case of Jimmy, when he reached the age of eight and entered the third grade, he began having some difficulty navigating the complex social interactions between his classmates and he began complaining, for example, about feeling alienated from different groups of kids on the playground. He would talk about his feelings some of the time, but not as often as he would in his earlier years, and I became concerned that he would have no outlet for these feelings.

During this period, Dave and I also saw a considerable increase in the general level of Jimmy's anxiety. While we tried to entice Jimmy to talk about what might be bothering him, he seemed increasingly tacit and resistant to opening up with us. We decided that he was probably entering an age where it was "uncool" to confide in his parents about matters of a social nature, and figured that an outside counselor might be better equipped to help him. Also, it seemed a good idea to have a professional therapist in the wings who was well versed in the intricacies of Jimmy's neurological profile.

Knowing what we did (and do) about the evolution of NLD—that a child does not "outgrow" the disorder and that, as an NLD child matures, he will begin to face different challenges as different social pressures begin to surface—we felt that two forms of outside help would be in order for Jimmy:

- *a psychologist or therapist*—a professional available who would know Jimmy's history and, more importantly, whom we could turn to in the event of a crisis situation arising. The last thing we needed was to have to get someone up to speed on Jimmy's history on very short notice.

- *a social skills training group*—to help him conquer some of his social awkwardness and to learn different ways to cope with social interactions both in school and outside school.

You may be wondering why this would be necessary since, as part of your child's IEP, he would be receiving similar services in the school setting. Well, the answer is that it may not be. You may be perfectly happy with the program of care that your child is receiving and, for a variety of reasons (not least of which is financial), you may choose not to have private therapy for your child. However, if you find that the therapists connected with the school are not properly educated or experienced about NLD or have not, in your estimation, developed an adequate plan of intervention, then you may want to look for outside help.

How do you find a good therapist for your child? To start, you get on the phone and do some networking (Whitney 2002). Some good calls to make would be the following:

- *the local learning disabilities association:* talk with the people there about your child's diagnosis and whom they might recommend who has experience in that area. You would be surprised at the wealth of information you can get by just asking these people.

- *your child's pediatrician:* he or she will at least be able to refer you to some local therapists and counselors who specialize in learning disabilities and even perhaps in NLD.

- *your state's department of education:* explain your situation and ask what resources they have, as well as the American Occupational Therapy Association or the National Association of Speech Therapists.

In nearly every community, there will be some kind of parent support network and, once you locate it, you're on your way. As I've discussed in the previous chapter, a SEPTA is a great way to become connected to other parents with special needs children, and through talking with them you can gather loads of information about therapists and different programs that are available to help your child.

How to choose a therapist

Choosing a therapist to help your NLD child is a task just like any other—well, maybe it's just a little more stressful than picking a plumber, because there's more at stake than a clogged drain here. You really don't want to screw this up. Just like with plumbers, there are good ones, bad ones, trained ones, untrained ones and just about everything in between. So how in the world do you pick? Well, you start by asking around about them before you even consider one, and then you talk to them on the phone and ask some basic questions to assess qualifications before you even come close to bringing your child in to see them. These questions might include the following:

1. Have you heard of NLD? If so, what do you know and where have you gathered your information? See if you agree with the thoughts as they are explained.

2. Ask about the therapist's training and certification. This will give you some indication of her specialties and experience.

3. Ask what frame of reference she uses to diagnose and treat. Therapists who work with NLD children should have a sensory integration frame of reference, meaning they have some training in treating the sensory processing piece of this disorder, which research indicates is a key element of treatment. They must know how to listen and relate to the needs of the NLD child.

4. Speech therapists should be able to demonstrate to you that they're competent in pragmatics and language, receptive language skills, and speed of processing of language and not just speech articulation.

5. Psychotherapists or psychologists need a proficiency in understanding nonverbal language, too, and use various methods, not just medication or behavioral theory.

6. Ask the therapist how long she generally sees a child and what her caseload currently is.

Beyond the obvious things that you should look for in a therapist—that they be caring and kind people who work well with children and that sincerely like being with them—a therapist must really value the role the parents play in the situation. While the therapist certainly has expertise and training which is what you are seeking from them, we as parents bring something very valuable to the table as well: our intuitive knowledge and deep love for our child. We are the ones that know our children the very best. We know what makes them tick, what makes them happiest, saddest, what tickles their funny bones. We're there for the daily ups and downs and all the in betweens. If the therapist that you interview is not willing to incorporate this into the treatment, then this probably isn't the best therapist to work with your child. Any therapist that you choose must:

- be kind and patient and demonstrate an unconditionally positive attitude

- behave respectfully toward your child

- be a good listener

- incorporate the things that you tell them into your child's treatment, or explain their reasons for not doing so

- make progress with your child

- have a good sense of humor

- be willing to interface with the special education staff at the school whenever necessary.

Whenever an issue arises that Jimmy is particularly upset about, I might not find out about it until we are on our way to Doug's (his psychologist's) office. In that case, I will ask to have a moment of Doug's time before Jimmy goes in, ostensibly to talk about a billing question (I seriously wonder how long before Jimmy catches on to this). But on a regular basis, Doug and I have an understanding that I can leave him a voicemail during the week that explains an issue or problem which has arisen that should be discussed during his session. Likewise, Jimmy knows that anything that is discussed with Doug during his session is confidential and will not be discussed with Dave or me.

Occupational therapy

When Jimmy was four years old, he began a course of treatment in occupational therapy with Debra Jablonski, OTR/L, BCP, in Danbury, CT, to increase his gross and fine motor skills as well as to strengthen his upper body/trunk area. He attended sessions twice a week for nearly two years, during which time he engaged in several different types of activities with his therapist including the following:

- jumping on a mini trampoline

- walking on a balance beam

- steadying himself while sitting on a t-bar type of seat and then tossing small bean bags at a cardboard brick wall

- lying tummy side down on a skateboard type device and then navigating his way across the room through a kind of obstacle course where he would have to pick up objects on the floor along the way while following lines and steering himself around cones

- sitting on a large inflated "physioball' while doing an activity such as playing catch with Debbie

- Debbie would hide pennies or tiddly winks into a substance like very hard Silly Putty™ and Jimmy would have to find them

- reaching into a large bowl filled with raw rice and finding small coins or clothes pins, then manipulating the pins onto the edge of the bowl

- swinging back and forth, tummy down, in a large net and having to throw bean bags at some target, either stacked cardboard bricks or boxes

- using scissors to cut different shapes out of paper

- copying shapes, drawing lines in a maze while trying to keep in between the lines, general work on penmanship (keeping his writing proportioned, well spaced, etc.).

Debbie was wonderful about changing around Jimmy's therapy routine to make it fun and interesting for him. She also attended meetings at his school, and offered suggestions as to ways to help him in the classroom:

- Proper positioning to encourage good posture—Jimmy should be seated in a chair that allows his feet to rest comfortably on the floor (hips and knees at approximately 90 degree angles).

- Jimmy may do well with a tilted table for added support when writing. To reproduce this in the classroom, you can try a three-ring binder as a surface for writing. Tilt the binder toward Jimmy and clip the paper to the surface with a large metal clip to prevent the paper from slipping.

- Jimmy should be seated in the front of the class with his body facing forward. He is easily distracted by extraneous visual stimuli, and this will help to diminish distractions from movement within the room.

- Jimmy tends to "sink" into his chair when seated for a long period of time. If this happens, he may need to stand or walk around for a few minutes. He would be a good candidate for errands (walking down to the office to deliver something, erasing the board, handing out supplies to students, etc.).

- Jimmy has a weakness of the small muscles of his hands, and he often needs cueing to hold the pencil properly. He uses a quadruple grasp (four fingers in contact with the pencil instead of three, as long as he maintains an open space between his thumb and first finger). He also has rubber or plastic grips that go over the pencil.

- Jimmy may also need some verbal cues to help him remember to hold the paper steady with his left hand when writing, as this does not always come naturally for him.

Debbie also gave me some activities that we could do at home with Jimmy to increase his upper body strength, and we did these religiously. Exercises like wheelbarrows, where I would hold his legs and he would have to scramble down the hallway using only his arms to mobilize himself. He found it to be difficult, but also very funny, and it was a fabulous way to strengthen his upper body. Another exercise was a simple modified push up which I could do right along with him. Jimmy was used to seeing his mom and dad do push ups in our downstairs gym, so he found it fun to do this sort of thing with us. We would also let Jimmy pick up our hand weights from time to time and do arm lifts (as long as he had on some sturdy shoes and we were close by spotting him).

Jimmy loved to go to O/T, and I think he was genuinely sad when he was discharged from therapy. He and Debbie had a great relationship, and we were very sad that we wouldn't be seeing her lovely smile every week. It's a bonus when you can make such good friends during this NLD journey.

Social skills training

As Jimmy entered the fourth grade, the issue of social skills moved to the forefront for a few reasons, one of which was that the girls in his class had all apparently taken some kind of potion over the summer which turned them into some of the most ornery pains in the butt you'd ever want to come across. Girls that Jimmy was good friends with in the third grade suddenly not only wanted nothing to do with him, but were going out of their way to be nasty and vindictive, as if his mere presence offended them. It was uncanny, but somehow not unbelievable (I was, after all, in fourth grade at one time myself). I tried to explain to my wounded son that girls can "be that way sometimes" but his muddled expression only made me feel worse for him, so I defaulted to "Why don't you just leave them alone and stick with your boy buddies?"

To add to his misery, Jimmy had also developed an unfortunate phobia of bees. It got to the point where he would refuse to go outside to play in the summer for fear that the bright flowers or the heat would attract these types of insects. Even if we were to go out in the car, Jimmy would have to exit the house by a certain door so that he didn't pass by any flowers or bushes. It was exhausting for him and also worrisome for us.

Now, you might wonder where social skills training would come into play here. Well, consider how such frenzy might affect him, say, on the playground. I can't say that his running around in circles and screaming at the top of his lungs because he hears a buzzing sound (remember his hyperacusis—hypersensitive hearing?) of a bee hovering over some clover 50 feet away is going to encourage the girls to say nicer things to him, do you? Okay, so given all that I was seeing and hearing about Jimmy's experiences, I thought that a social skills training group made up of his peers might not be a bad idea.

Enter Superkids, a program in Ridgefield (a neighboring town) run by social workers and child psychologists. The purpose of the program is to build social skills and positive connections among the children in its groups. Jimmy's good friend Jack, whom I described earlier in the book, had participated in many of the Superkids social skills training groups and his parents had spoken very highly of them. The program also offers summer camp as well as a "get ready for school' week during the summer to help kids work through some of the stress of the first few weeks of school.

Let me just say that Jimmy did not want to go to Superkids. He was perfectly happy going to see Doug once a week, and he could not understand why he had to go talk to other kids about stuff that he already talked to Doug about. To say he was resistant doesn't even come close to describing the grief he was giving me all the way to our first appointment. But we were going, and that was it. I just prayed that he wasn't going to sit tight-lipped at the intake and waste everyone's time. If he did, I figured it wouldn't be the first time this had happened, and the counselor might just have to earn her money that day.

When we arrived at the intake, our interviewer, Barbara, knew immediately that Jimmy was on edge and extremely skeptical about the whole idea. The dialogue went something like this.

Barbara: Hi Jimmy, my name is Barbara.

Jimmy: Hey.

[Jimmy began looking at the television set in the office.]

Barbara: Do you like television?

Jimmy: I don't really like to watch it. But I like them.

Barbara: Oh, you like the insides of them?

Jimmy: Yeah.

[Jimmy perked up.]

Barbara: What about the insides of them do you like?

Jimmy: Everything. The wires and all the lights and stuff.

Barbara: You know, we have other kids in our groups who like that too.

Jimmy: Hmmm.

Barbara: Is there anything you really don't like?

Jimmy: Bees. I really don't like them.

Barbara: Do they scare you?

Jimmy: Yeah. A lot.

Barbara: Do they scare you when you're outside or even when you're inside?

Jimmy: They scare me all the time.

Barbara: You know we have a boy in one of our groups that is so afraid of birds that he doesn't want to go outside. So we know all about being afraid of things here, and the kids can talk about that stuff together. It helps.

Jimmy: But birds won't hurt you.

Barbara: He thinks they will.

She had won him over in less than five minutes. The conversation went on for a while, and then Barbara invited Jimmy to go into another room to play a game. He went willingly. Shortly thereafter, I enrolled Jimmy in one of the groups with four or five other fourth graders.

According to the information given to me by Barbara, during the sessions the children will do a lot of role playing to learn social skills tactics and learn ways to problem solve. They will also be able to freely talk about issues that may arise in school and offer their views to each other as well as enlist the help of the therapist that is overseeing the group. During the session, there is also free time when the kids can interact and do a relaxing craft or other project together. Friendships are formed and trust is built during the group, and it is a safe place for the kids to express themselves.

A helpful by-product of the social skills training group is that it offers a social venue in which the NLD child can both function and be observed that is quite apart from the school or any other environment that he participates in during the normal course. It's kind of like a controlled social experiment, if you will. If there are certain issues or behaviors, for example, that your child seems to be grappling with, you can bring them to the attention of the group counselors and they can, in turn, weave them into a weekly session. Since these groups are generally kept small in number (no more than seven), there is plenty of attention for each child.

Perhaps one of the more obvious advantages of a group such as the one that Jimmy attends weekly at Superkids is that, given the fact that children will tend to be placed by age and (more or less) by level of social ability, it would stand to reason that the counselors overseeing these groups would have the advantage of evaluating your NLD child's social skills and other coping strategies. Their capacity to do so clearly transcends the immediate group your child participates in to include the entire universe of children that these folks come in contact with, both learning disabled and typical. This can prove exceedingly helpful and productive, as it gives the parent a concrete point of reference.

After Jimmy had participated in Superkids for four months, Dave and I had our first parent conference with his counselors. The first surprise was that conferences were offered on Saturday to accommodate parents that work outside of the home. The second surprise was the length and breadth of the conference itself: Dave and I expected to have a short chat with Jimmy's counselor, basically about how he was playing with the other kids. What we got, however, was something quite different, and a far sight more valuable. The counselor gave us an overview of Jimmy's strengths with respect to the group as a whole, which was a perfect way to begin the conference. She emphasized how he made a real effort to nurture friendships with the other kids in the group and how it was apparent to her that this was an important social activity to him, pointing out that this was quite a milestone for an NLD child (and how often children in these groups show no incentive at all to initiate friendships). She gave us many specific examples from copious notes that she had in front of her, of things that Jimmy had done in session or of different situations involving him to illustrate points that she was making, and we found this to be exceedingly helpful and enlightening. She also gave us ample opportunity to add our own insights as well as to ask questions.

She then came around to the issue of Jimmy's anxiety, which was something that Dave and I had been fully aware of but hadn't really addressed directly for some time. (Note: while anxiety is common in the NLD child, the level exhibited by Jimmy may not be.) It had been brought up during prior PPTs at the school as well as with Jimmy's private psychologist, and we had all tried to come up with various strategies through which Jimmy could relieve his anxiety. These included various stress-reducing exercises like holding squeeze balls or putty, gum chewing, breathing exercises, etc. Jimmy either didn't want to use these tactics or they simply didn't work. We were finding that his anxiety was worsening and was leading to disfluency in his speech (stammering), moodiness and irritability which was putting some strain on the household dynamic and, most importantly, undue stress and strain on Jimmy. He would fly off the handle at the littlest thing and just couldn't seem to regroup from the slightest disappointment or aggravation. He was suffering unnecessarily, and this was becoming increasingly apparent to Dave and I. But hearing it from a third party, someone who wasn't part of our inner circle and wasn't a teacher, somehow made it crystal clear that perhaps it was time to consider some anti-anxiety medication for our son to help relieve him of some of his discomfort. We then took the information from the conference and consulted with Jimmy's private psychologist who concurred with the high level of anxiety that they observed and was supportive of the idea of trying to relieve it through medication. We are in the process of finding a suitable pediatric psychiatrist to work with so that Jimmy will be able to feel a little better in his "skin."

Summary

1.   Seeking professional counseling or therapy for the NLD child is sometimes helpful with some of the social, motor and/or emotional problems that manifest themselves, particularly as the child gets older and becomes less inclined to open up with his parents.

2.   Local learning disabilities associations, pediatricians and/or state departments of education may be good sources for names/recommendations of therapists.

3.   Choosing the right therapist is important. Find one who is caring and kind, who likes children and, preferably, one who has experience with or knowledge of NLD.

4.   Occupational therapy can be used to increase gross and fine motor skills in the NLD child, a common problem. The occupational therapist should be experienced with LD children and be willing to make the therapy fun and interesting for a child.

5.   Social skills training groups can help the child learn, through role play and discussion, appropriate behaviors in social situations such as in the classroom, on the playground, at parties, etc. A helpful by-product of these groups is that they offer a social venue in which the NLD child can both function and be observed that is quite apart from the school or any other environment that he participates in during the normal course.

Chapter 15

Looking Ahead

I still remember thinking, when reading the words "nonverbal learning disability" in reference to my son Jimmy, that there was something wrong with him. Today, five years later, I have come to accept Jimmy's NLD diagnosis as something quite different: Jimmy is a nine-year-old boy with his own unique set of gifts and challenges that require understanding and support so that he can realize his full potential. There is nothing whatsoever wrong with him. He, indeed, has a special kind of brain and, therefore, requires a special kind of understanding by those that cross his path. I suppose that 50 years ago, before dedicated folks like Dr. Byron Rourke studied syndromes such as NLD, there probably were children just like Jimmy who were terribly misunderstood, perhaps even labeled as less capable than others. That's a terribly sad thought, but it makes me believe that, in the years to come, we will only better understand about learning differences and, more importantly, about how we can better adapt teaching methods to the variances in brain function that naturally occur from one individual to the next.

In our family, we have learned a great deal about Jimmy over the past five years, as I'm sure he has about himself. My son has grown from an antisocial four-year-old to a boy who wants to nurture friendships and is trying to navigate his way in a complex social world. As parents, we find ourselves trying to find the right balance between staying involved and accessible while also allowing Jimmy the latitude he needs to grow— always a difficult task but a particularly difficult one with the NLD child where the tendency is to overprotect. As Jimmy faces middle school in the fall, he will probably only want to push us away more.

In writing this book, I have had the opportunity to revisit many of the experiences that I have had with Jimmy and those that we have

shared as a family. There have been many trying times and many glorious ones. Dave and I have made the best decisions we could for our son, and we have always tried, as Dr. Rourke advised us, to "imagine what the world must seem like to Jimmy." It has helped us immeasurably in our parenting, and we have given the same advice to many other parents along the way. All in all, the journey has been an inspirational one, one which I would neither want to change nor, in all honesty, repeat. I'm happy to have done it, however, and I'm looking forward to continuing.

Looking ahead, the teenage years will present new challenges as puberty, peer pressure, girls, and all that goes with them erupt (help!). We will also face many new areas of independence for Jimmy as he begins to drive, enters the world of after-school work and begins to look at universities. That should be fodder for another volume or two (if I survive, that is). In the meantime, I hope that my reflections, advice, insights and ramblings have provided some help and support to those of you who are either new to the world of NLD or are simply looking for another parent's view.

Here's to all of you parents, caregivers, and anyone who touches the life of an NLD child, who cares enough to want to understand him a little bit better. Here's to all of the special brains.

In 2001, I wrote and recorded original music for a CD entitled *On and On*. One of the songs on that CD was inspired by my son Jimmy and his journey with NLD. These are the lyrics to that song.

Willy

Can I sit with you
I have worries too
Oh but we can talk a while
Let's walk a million miles
We'll make 'em understand
Just let me hold your hand

Blossoms on the trees
Swingin' in the breeze
They're flying high for you
For everything you do
Is like a melody
My heart can sing along with me

Sing your song, boy
Just the way you hear it
Life's a ride, boy
You've got to steer it
Don't fear it

Here we go again
Half way 'round the bend
We're just misunderstood
Need a new neighborhood
But keep your eye on me
And set your spirit free

Willy Willy Willy
We've got a row to hoe
Let's take it nice and slow
So many things they don't know
Willy Willy Willy
Don't change a single thing for me.

Epilogue

This book is dedicated to my father, Calvin D. Russell, who was diagnosed with a brain tumor in November, 2003, just a few months before its completion. The weeks that ensued were terribly worrisome ones filled with hospital stays, testing, surgery and the like. My father was eventually diagnosed with glioblastoma multiforme, a terminal form of brain cancer. He died on January 5, 2004, one day short of two months from the date of his diagnosis. He was 71 years old.

My father was, in my not so humble estimation, a man well ahead of his time. He never considered there a limit to the aspirations of his daughters nor did he ever, in the slightest manner, make reference to gender as an impediment to any goal that my sister or I had set in our sights, no matter how lofty. He had a great distaste for conformity, yet embraced with relish any desire to be different, to "stir things up," and would always encourage me to do just that. For instance, in reference to a rather large rock nestled in the front lawn of my childhood home, Dad said that, while many people would remove the rock, he believed that "when you have something different, rather than remove it, you should feature it." He planted a lovely forsythia bush next to the rock and every spring the area was abloom with his philosophy that "different is good."

My father was a teacher from the moment he rose in the morning to his last kiss on my forehead upon tucking me in at night. He was a voracious reader and knew endless facts about things I could only begin to marvel at: occurrences in the deepest parts of the ocean, the types of gases in the rings around Saturn, how glue really works. The first inspiration behind my writing, he encouraged me to read *The Grapes of Wrath* by John Steinbeck as a young girl, and I was entirely overwhelmed by the book, reduced to tears by the final scene when the grown, starving man feeds from the bulging breast of a young woman. I remember talking to my dad for weeks after reading that book, about the Okies, the Dust Bowl and the Depression. I was impressed not only by the story itself but by the manner in which words, when put together so beautifully yet so simply (as Steinbeck did), could leave such a lasting impression. These are just some of the gifts my father gave me.

When grandchildren came along, Dad shared this love with them by spending summer afternoons teaching them the habits of bumblebees or guiding them through the raspberry bushes in his backyard garden. I will forever savor the image of my dad holding the hand of one grand-child or the other as he lumbered along the grass, leaning down in con-versation about one fact or another.

Dad loved to talk to Jimmy, and found his concise, literal view of things very refreshing. He took a lot of time to talk to Jimmy and, just as importantly, to let him talk back, to listen carefully to him. I remember particularly how the two of them enjoyed greeting each other by speaking the other's name backwards. My father would come into our house with a huge smile and say, "Hi, Ymmij Regrub!" And Jimmy would shout back gleefully, "Hey, Nivlac Llessur!"

It is difficult, impossible in fact, to describe the loss that my father's passing means to my life—nor is that the purpose of this epilogue. But I can say with some resolve that perhaps the greatest lesson I learned from my father has been that I was loved and accepted precisely as I was from the very first, unconditionally, completely, and unwaveringly. It made for a beautiful life, one for which I will be forever grateful, and it is a lesson that I will happily pass on to my children.

I love you, Dad, and I will miss you every single day.

Acknowledgments

Before I express the heartfelt gratitude that is long overdue to the scads of people who supported me through the writing of this book, I feel I must first acknowledge Dr. Byron Rourke for putting the seed in my head to write it in the first place. When Dave and I sat in his office back in May of 2001, we were literally on the edges of our seats, hanging on his every word as he discussed this strange new world of nonverbal learning disability and what it meant to our son's life. He was very interested in our lives and what our world was as well, and when he found out that I was a writer by profession, he encouraged me to consider writing a book about the journey of parenting a child with NLD. I am very grateful for his encouragement and support, for this has indeed been a wonderfully fulfilling journey for me and for my family, and one that I hope will prove helpful to many others.

My thanks and love go to the following people:

- my husband David, for your unconditional love and tireless care, for your timely sense of humor, for having to constantly jog your memory on the spur of the moment, and for enduring countless nights of bad dinners and little or no company—I love you dearly

- my precious children Jimmy and Shawn, for putting stars in my eyes, moons in my skies and songs in my soul—you are the best part of my life

- my sister Judy, for your support, encouragement, suggestions, and for the countless hours spent reading, editing and organizing when crunch time came—your help has meant the world to me

- my mother and father, for always believing in me and loving me just the way I am

- Emily, Elizabeth, and Jack, for the joy you bring to my heart

- my brother-in-law Tom, thanks for your interest in all that I do—it means a lot

- our extended family who have followed this journey from the beginning—we love you

- my friends who have listened and understood and cheered me on—I love you all.

I would also like to extend my deepest appreciation and gratitude to:

- Joan Cone, a dear friend to me and to Jimmy and a truly gifted and dedicated teacher—we cherish how real you are

- the entire Special Services Staff and Administration at Redding Elementary School, especially Chris Hannafey, Ingrid Erikson, Bev O'Boza, Phyllis Conley and Mary Lou Torre—ours is an incredible journey, and I'm glad we're taking it together

- Diane DeBonis, Rebecca McClure and Chris Wermuth, Jimmy's extraordinary teachers at Redding Elementary School: I hope you know the difference that you make every single day

- Pat Kelley and Steve McCullough, for being such great friends to Jimmy

- the entire staff at RES Extended Day—for taking great care of our kids

- Christian Russo (a real legend in the Burger household), thanks for taking the time to understand Jimmy

- Drs. Humberto Bauta and Laura Nowacki, for the dedication and care you have always given and continue to provide to my children and for having the foresight to send us to the people at CCMC

- Debbie Jablonski, OTR/L, BCP, for all the ways you've helped Jimmy and so many children

- Kevin Daly of the Connecticut PTA—you've been a wonderful support and a great inspiration to me

- Doug Scarth, PhD, for your care, dedication, and memory of sports facts

- the entire staff at Superkids in Danbury, Connecticut—yours is a wonderful mission, and we're so grateful that you've chosen it.

Resources

Websites

www.allkindsofminds.org
All Kinds of Minds is a nonprofit organization formed to further the understanding of learning differences. The site focuses on increasing the understanding and support for children with learning differences, and is based upon the work of Dr. Mel Levine and his colleagues.

www.ideapractice.org
Special education law as well as questions, answers and links to other sources are all provided in this site which is sponsored by the Council for Exceptional Children Leadership Initiative.

www.ncld.org
This site, which promotes public awareness and understanding of children and adults with learning disabilities, has many full test articles and excellent links to additional learning disability resources.

www.neuropsychologycentral.com
This site explains the details associated with neuropsychological testing, how to find a tester and what questions to ask.

www.NLDA.org
This is the official website of the Nonverbal Learning Disorder Association.

www.NLDline.com
This original website on NLD is devoted to increasing awareness of the disorder among parents and professionals. The site features articles, personal stories as well as a penpals section for children with NLD.

www.nldontheweb.org
This is the most comprehensive NLD site on the web and is the official web presence of Dr. Byron Rourke as well as the world wide web headquarters of Sue Thompson, MA, CET. The site is large but easy to navigate and provides information for parents, professionals and educators alike.

www.schwablearning.org
This site provides free information, resources, publications and support through two websites:

www.schwablearning.org offers a parent's guide to helping children with learning disabilities; while www.SparkTop.org was created expressly for kids ages 8 to 12 who struggle with learning difficulties.

www.theideabox.com
This site has great activity ideas to promote learning from teachers and therapists.

www.wrightslaw.com
This site provides information on educational law and advocacy. You'll find hundreds of articles, cases, newsletters and other information about special education law.

Organizations

Learning Disabilities Association of America (LDA)
4156 Library Road
Pittsburgh, PA 15234
USA
(888) 300-6710
(412) 341-1515
(412) 341-8077
email: *ldanatl@usaor.net*
web: *www.ldanatl.org*

National Center for Learning Disabilities (NCLD)
381 Park Avenue South, Suite 1401
New York, NY 10016
USA
(888) 575-7373
(212) 545-7510
web: *www.ncld.org*

Nonverbal Learning Disorders Association
PO Box 220
Canton, CT 06019-0220
USA
(860) 693-3738
email: *NLDA@nlda.org*
web: *www.nlda.org*

Office of Special Education and Rehabilitative Services
Clearinghouse on Disability Information
Room 3132, Switzer Building
330 C Street S.W.
Washington DC 20202-2524
USA
(202) 205-8241
web: *www.ed.gov/offices/OSERS*

Bibliography

Bateman, B. and Herr, C. (2003) *Writing Measurable IEP Goals and Objectives.* Verona, WI: Attainment Publications. (www.AttainmentCompany.com)

Bates, L. (1985) *Your Three-Year-Old, Friend or Enemy.* New York: Dell Publishers. (www.randomhouse.com/bantamdell)

Bérard, G. (1993) *Hearing Equals Behavior.* New Canaan, CT: Keats Publishing.

Cutler, B.C. (1993) *You, Your Child, and Special Education: A Guide to Making the System Work.* Baltimore, MD: Brookes.

Duke, M.P., Nowicki, S. and Martin, E.A. (1996) *Teaching Your Child the Language of Social Success.* Atlanta, GA: Peachtree Publishers. (Www.peachtreeonline.com)

Kranowitz, M.A. (1998) *The Out-of-Sync Child: Recognizing and Coping with Sensory Integration Dysfunction.* New York: Penguin Putnam. (www.penguinputnam.com)

Rogers, F. (2003) *The World According to Mister Rogers.* New York: Hyperion. (www.hyperion.com)

Rourke, B. (ed.) (1995) *Syndrome of Nonverbal Learning Disabilities: Neurodevelopmental Manifestations.* New York: Guilford Press.

Stewart, K. (2002) *Helping a Child with Nonverbal Learning Disorder or Asperger's Syndrome: A Parent's Guide.* Oakland, CA: New Harbinger Publications. (www.newharbinger.com)

Tanguay, P. (2001) *Nonverbal Learning Disabilities at Home: A Parent's Guide.* London: Jessica Kingsley Publishers. (www.jkp.com)

Tanguay, P. (2002) *Nonverbal Learning Disabilities at School: Educating Students with NLD, Asperger Syndrome, and Related Conditions.* London: Jessica Kingsley Publishers. (www.jkp.com)

Thompson, S.T. (1997) *The Source for Nonverbal Learning Disorders.* East Moline, IL: LinguiSystems. (www.linguisystems.com)

Whitney, R.V. (2002) *Bridging the Gap: Raising a Child with Nonverbal Learning Disorder.* New York: Berkley Publishing Group. (www.penguinputnam.com)

Wright, P. and Wright, P. (2002a) *From Emotions to Advocacy: The Special Education Survival Guide.* Hartfield, VA: Harbor House Law Press.

Wright, P. and Wright, P. (2002b) *Wrightslaw: Special Education Law.* Hartfield, VA: Harbor House Law Press.

Index

abstract reasoning 129
academic work 127–30
   difficult areas 33, 129
   strengths 33, 128
   see also homework; schools
activities for the NLD child 112–23
   bike rides 116–17
   hiking 113–14, 123
   household chores 120
   ice skating 119
   indoor activities 119–20
   music 114–15, 123
   playground games 115
   and problems with television/computer games 121
   riding 113
   running 118
   shooting hoops 114
   swimming 116
   team sports 113
adaptability 24
adaptive functioning 34
advocacy roles 38–9
   dealing with teachers and other professionals 125–7, 164–6
   preparing for/participating in meetings 131–6
   and self-advocacy for NLD children 148–9
   and siblings 55
amusement parks 61, 173–4
anxiety
   fixations as coping mechanism 82–3
   manifestations in NLD children 16, 22, 26
   and medication 206–7
   parental 11, 13, 94
   and stress-reducing tactics 206–7
   terrors and fears 72–4, 81–2, 202–3
anxiety reactions
   and fixations 82–3
   hysteria and "meltdowns" 48–9, 72–4, 81, 202–3

apologizing, for parenting "mistakes" 168–9
appearances
   body image 107–8
   dress sense 107
   personal hygiene 108, 157–8
argumentative behaviors 87–8
Asperger's Syndrome 160
assessment centers 32
   diagnostic evaluations 32–6
   information resources and contact details 216
   Superkids (social skills training) 206
attention and concentration problems 32–3
attention deficit hyperactivity disorder (ADHD), possible links with immunizations 19
"attention seeking" behaviors 22
auditory stimulation, and acute sensitivity to sounds 73–4, 203

behavioral problems *see* anxiety reactions; fixations; social skill deficits
bike rides 116–17
birthdays 67–8
body image, and dangers of fixation 107–8
body space awareness 99
books and literature, information sources 41, 101, 167, 217
bowel problems, constipation 156–8
brain development, and white matter abnormalities 17–18
breathing exercises 206
Bridging the Gap: Raising a Child with Nonverbal Learning Disorder (Whitney) 41
brothers and sisters 53–5, 152–3
bullying 90, 140–1
   strategies to deal with situations 141
   see also appearances

changes to normal routine
   coping with unexpected situations 60, 62–3
   doctor's visits/medical appointments 95–6
   "new" teachers/babysitters/doctors 97
   redecorating 96, 163–4
chewing reflex 158
childhood immunizations, studies on possible links to NLD 19
choices
   facilitating decision-making 62
   problems with over-stimulation 58–9

KISS (Keep It Simple, Silly) 64–5

Christmas 176–8

"clumsiness" 20–1

communication with NLD children 23–4

advice and guidance 35

and "transitioning" difficulties 21, 26, 161–3

being specific 46, 50

inability to read nonverbal communication signs 34, 87–8

keeping things "literal" 23–4, 35, 46, 50, 167–8

practising conversation and language skills 51–2

prompting and verbal cueing 32

see also social skills training

community support see parent support groups; Special Education Parent Teacher Association (SEPTA)

computer games/videos 121

managing excessive playing 121

use on vacations 172

condominiums/self catering vacations 171–2

conformity, of appearance 107–8

Connecticut Association for Children and Adults with Learning Disabilities (CACLD) 132

Connecticut Children's Medical Center (CCMC) 32

constipation 156–8

conversation skills 103–4

prompting and verbal cueing 32

rehearsal and practice 51–2, 104, 204

coordination difficulties 20–1

cues and prompts 35

learning appropriate responses 102–3

use of written instructions 139

verbal prompts 32, 202

decision-making

facilitating choices 62

and KISS (Keep It Simple, Silly) 64–5

problems with over-stimulation 21, 58–9

see also parenting

diagnosis

assessment and evaluation processes 32–6

dealing with diagnosis 13–14, 36–42

and discussing NLD with your child 144–55

manifestations and signs prior to diagnosis 29–32

problems with misdiagnosis 25

and telling family/friends 167

diagnostic investigations 32–5

perceptual/cognitive assessments 32–3

psychological/behavioral observations 33–5

diagonals, inability to perceive 26

diaries and notebooks 37–8, 125–6

diet, and food dislikes 158–9

disability

concepts according to Rogers 147

discussions with your NLD child 144–8, 149

using alternative words 153–4

discipline 45–8

discovery learning vs. verbal "labeling" 22, 24–5, 35, 160–1

discussing NLD with your child 144–55

disorganization 161–3

and school work 138

dress style, and peer conformity 107

education see academic work; learning styles; schools

educational programs see Individualized Educational Programs (IEPs)

emotional development 34–5

and instilling self-esteem 50

empathy 101–2

environmental changes 96

redecorating 96, 163–4

evaluation centers 32

diagnostic assessments 32–6

information resources and contact details 216

social skills 206

exams see tests

exercises

and stress relief 206

therapy for motoric disorders 20–1, 200–2

facial expressions 101–2

"smiley faces" used as grading system 136–7

see also nonverbal communication

families

sibling dynamics 53–5

as support networks 166–7

family celebrations 67–8, 90–1, 176–8

family outings

amusement parks 61, 173–4

holidays 63–4, 170–6, 176–9

importance of preparation and rehearsal 68–9

parties 59–60, 150

shopping 22, 58

weekends away 174–6

fears and terrors 72–4, 81–2, 202–3

field trips 141

fixations 52, 71–85

as anxiety-relief 82–3

coping mechanisms for parents 72, 82–4

duration 71

examples of situations 71–82

and *hyperacusis* 73–4

on mechanical objects 71–2, 77, 79–81

as opportunities for shared activities 121

with people 74–5, 77–9

and persistence 84

and phobias 72–4, 81–2

preparing for situations 83–4

with toys 75–7

food-related issues

chewing reflex 158

restricted diets 158–9

friendships 108–10, 206

"best" friends 108–10, 188–9

"buddying" arrangements 188–9

dependency on adults 22, 23

difficulties with peers 22–3, 31, 34–5, 42–3, 88, 91–4

and parental interventions 93–4, 189

rejection by peers 22, 92–3, 108–10, 202–3

and self-advocacy 149

see also social skill deficits; social skills training

gender differentials 20

genetic basis for NLD 18–19

grooming 108

group therapy work/play sessions 203–7

hearing, acute sensitivity to sounds 73–4

Helping a Child with Nonverbal Learning Disorder or Asperger's Syndrome (Stewart) 41

hiking/walking 113–14, 123

holidays 63–4, 170–6, 176–9

and doing nothing 178–9

and familiar routines 172–4

and family traditions 177–8

hotels vs. condominiums (self-catering) 171–2

vacations 170–6

weekends away 174–6

homework 138–9

helpful tips 130–1

horse riding 113

hospitality 105

household chores 120

difficulties for the NLD child 161–3

teaching organizational skills 162–3

hyperacusis 73–4, 203

hysteria and "meltdowns", as reaction to phobias 48–9, 72–4, 81, 202–3

ice skating 119

immunizations, studies on possible links to NLD 19

impulsiveness 99–101

see also routines

incidence of NLD 20

Individualized Educational Programs (IEPs) 39, 129–30, 135–6

how to get the most from meetings 132–3, 134, 135–6

pre-meeting checklists 134

see also advocacy roles; planning and placement team (PPT)

indoor play activities 119–20

information sources

books and literature 41, 101, 167, 217

for children 193, 205

local SEPTA groups 40, 189–95

organizations 40, 189–95, 216

websites 41, 148, 193, 215–16

information/sensory overload, coping strategies 58–69

Institute of Medicine (IOM), studies on safety of childhood immunizations 19

Internet, as source of information 36–7, 41

KISS (Keep It Simple, Silly) 64–5

language abilities 16–17, 34

and literal interpretations 23–4, 160–1

significance in learning development for NLD
    children 160–1
and white matter brain damage 18
language use
importance of literal speech 23, 167–8
see also communication with NLD children
laxatives 156–7
learning styles
    and academic work 128–9
    and cognitive flexibility 33–4
    differences between NLD and NT children 160
    discovery learning vs. verbal "labeling" 22,
        24–5, 33, 35, 160–1
    importance of literal speech 23, 35, 46, 50,
        167–8
    see also communication with NLD children
legal aspects 193
literature, book recommendations 41, 217
long-term memory, information retrieval 33, 128,
    168
losses 185–6

manifestations and signs 15–16, 20–5, 26
    motoric disorders 20–1, 30
    social disorders 22–3
    visual-spatial (organizational) disorders 21–2
    see also fixations; social skill deficits
mealtimes 158–9
media and news, managing inflow 66–7
medication 207
"meltdowns" 48–9
memory skills
    and difficulties with concentration 33
    information retrieval abilities 33, 128, 168
misdiagnosis 25
Mister Rogers' Neighborhood 146–8
modelling social skills 104, 204
    see also social skills training
monologues 22, 35, 87
    and lack of discovery learning abilities 24–5,
        160–1
motoric disorders 20–1, 30
    causes 17–18
    coping mechanisms 20–1
    fine motor coordination problems 33
    gross motor weaknesses 31, 33

therapeutic interventions 200–2
and upper body weakness 31
moving house 180–5
    tips for making it work 184–5
multitask instructions 21, 29
    and organizational difficulties 161–3
music 114–15, 123

"name calling" and "put-downs" 49
nonverbal communication 34, 87–8
    hostile/threatening reactions 106
    methods of teaching 101–2
*Nonverbal Learning Disabilities at Home: A Parent's
    Guide* (Tanguay) 41
Nonverbal Learning Disorder (NLD) 16–17
    biological basis 17–18
    causes 18–19
    defined 16–17
    discovery and identification of condition 17
    discussions with your child 144–6, 149–52,
        153–4
    incidence 20
    manifestations and signs 15–16, 20–5, 26, 30,
        161–3
    and misdiagnosis 25
    what to call condition 154
notebooks 37–8, 125–6
novelty
    celebrations 67–8, 90–1
    coping with unexpected situations 60, 62–3
    family outings 59–60, 61, 63–4, 68–9
    field trips 141
    see also routines
numeracy 33, 130

obsessions *see* fixations
occupational therapy
    activities for motoric disorders 20–1, 31,
        200–2
    in assessment of motoric responses 30–1
organizational skill deficits
    causes 17–18
    manifestations and signs 21–2, 34, 161–3

parent support groups 40
    getting involved 187–9

see also Special Education Parent Teacher
    Association (SEPTA)
parent-Special Services groups 192
parent/teacher associations
    and special educational needs support 40
    see also Planning and Placement Team (PPT);
        Special Education Parent Teacher
        Association (SEPTA)
parental reactions
    coping mechanisms 13–14, 37–42
    focusing on the positive 26–7
    impact of diagnosis 36
    importance of relaxing 41–2
    looking ahead 208–9
    to bullying 89–90, 140–1
parenting
    and advocacy 38–9, 124–5, 131–6, 164–6
    dealing with anxiety-induced extreme
        behaviors 48–9, 72–4, 81–2, 206–7
    discipline 45–8
    discussing NLD with your child 144–55
    finding time for partners 55–6
    having fun 65, 127
    instilling self-esteem 50, 146–8
    and overprotection 45, 89–90
    and patience 52–3
    providing perspective 179
    providing routine and stability 24, 35, 53, 141
    and relaxation 41, 127
    and siblings 53–5
    and teaching your child self-advocacy 149
    see also family outings
parties 59–60, 150
peers see friendships
perception difficulties 161
    diagonals 26
    and spatial awareness 99
perceptual/cognitive assessments 32–3
perseverations 52, 71–85
    as anxiety-relief 82–3
    coping mechanisms for parents 72, 82–5
    duration 71
    examples of situations 71–82
    and hyperacusis 73–4
    on mechanical objects 71–2, 77, 79–81
    with people 74–5, 77–9

and persistence 84
and phobias 72–4, 81–2, 202–3
preparing for situations 83–4, 204–7
with toys 75–7
personal hygiene 108
    and toileting problems 157–8
phobias 72–4, 81–2, 202–3
    and stress-reducing tactics 206–7
physical exercise, and motoric disorders 20–1
physical signs and manifestations
        motoric disorders 20–1, 30
        and upper body weakness 31
Planning and Placement Team (PPT) 124–5,
    126–7
        meetings 39, 131–6
        see also advocacy roles; Individualized
            Educational Programs (IEPs)
play acting
        fixations and imitation of characters 74–5,
        77–9
        see also role play
playing with peers 104–5
        bullying 90, 140–1
        role of parents 89
        in school 115
        and team sports 113
        see also activities for the NLD child; friendships;
            social skills training
positive reinforcement 50
problem areas see manifestations and signs
problem solving abilities 33, 129
prompts see cues and prompts
psychological/behavioral observations 33–5
psychologists, how to choose a therapist 198–200
"put-downs" 49

quantitative skills 33, 130

reactions to diagnosis
        families and friends 167
        parents 36
reading skills 128–9
recall see memory skills
record keeping 37–8, 125–6
"red flags" see manifestations and signs
redecorating 96, 163–4

relaxation 41, 127

relocation 180–5

   tips for making it work 184–5

reprimands 47–8

Rogers, Fred 146–8

role play 204

Rourke, Dr. Byron 17–20, 160–1

routines

   coping with unexpected situations 60, 62–3

   and doctor's visits/medical appointments 95–6

   and holidays 172–4

   importance to NLD children 24, 35

   problems with novelty/surprises 60, 62–3, 67–8, 90–1, 141, 150, 163–4, 180–5

school tests 129, 142

   and segregation 150–1

schools

   bullying 140–1

   changes and "new terms" 180–5

   communication of diagnosis 39–40

   coping with academic work 127–30

   field trips 141

   general advice for teachers 35–6

   getting to know staff 126–7

   and homework 130–1, 138–9

   and Individualized Educational Programs (IEPs) 39, 129–30, 132–3, 134, 135–6

   looking at different options 180–1

   marking/grading systems 136–7

   and organizational skill deficits 139

   tests 129, 142, 150–1

   see also friendships; learning styles; Special Education Parent Teacher Association (SEPTA)

seating systems 21

self-esteem in NLD children 50, 146–8

   see also bullying

sensory stimuli

   excessive inflow and overload 21–2, 58–9

   general principles of management 64–5

   methods of handling situations 59–64, 65–9

   see also hyperacusis; phobias

September 11, 2001 65–7

shoe laces 164–6

shopping 22, 58

short-term memory, and attention/concentration difficulties 32–3

siblings 53–5

   talking about NLD 152–3

signs of NLD *see* manifestations and signs

social competence 87

social judgements 106

social skill deficits 86–97

   causes 17–18, 86–8, 202–3

   manifestations and signs 22–3, 34–5

social skills training 36, 98–111, 202–7

   body space awareness 99

   conversation skills 103–4

   dealing with fears and phobias 202–7

   dealing with frustrations and impulses 99–101

   empathy 101–2

   and general appearance 106–8

   group sessions 202–7

   hospitality 105

   learning appropriate responses 102–3

   personal appearance 106–8

   play skills 104–5

   responding to threatening/hostile nonverbal clues 106

   role play 204

   and self-advocacy 149

   see also friendships

The Source for Nonverbal Learning Disorders (Thompson) 41, 167

spatial awareness

   and body space 99

   inability to perceive diagonals 26

   and organizational abilities 161

Special Education Law 193

Special Education Parent Teacher Association (SEPTA) 40, 189–95

   aims and goals 189–92

   getting started 191–2

   research and information sources 193

   seminars, workshops and conferences 192–3

   support and camaraderie 193–4

special occasions 67–8

   family celebrations 67–8, 90–1, 176–8

   see also family outings; holidays; surprises

spelling 128

sports and activities *see* activities

standardized tests 142
Stewart, K. 20
stimuli, and information/sensory overload 58–9
study skills 129, 130–1, 138–9
Superkids (Ridgefield) 203–7
support networks
    families and friends 166–7, 189
    parent support groups 40, 187–9
    teachers and other professionals 124–5,
        126–7, 131–6
    see also Special Education Parent Teacher
        Association (SEPTA); Superkids
        (Ridgefield)
supportive seating 21
surprises
    coping with unexpected situations 60, 62–3
    see also routines
swimming 116
symptoms see manifestations and signs

talking "nonstop" see monologues; verbal "labeling"
"talking back" 45–7, 91
teaching
    general advice on communication 35
    managing social skill deficits in NDL children
        88–9
    see also communication with NLD children;
        learning styles; schools
Teaching Your Child the Language of Social Success
    (Duke, Nowicki and Martin) 41, 101
team sports 113
teenagers 209
television and media
    managing excessive viewing 121
    managing inflow 66–7
    use in teaching social skills 102
    use on vacations 172
temporal concepts, difficulties for NLD children
    129, 160
tests 129, 142
    and segregation 150–1
therapeutic interventions 196–207
    choosing a therapist 198–200
    general advice on communication 35
    and learning programs 129–30
    occupational therapy 20–1, 30–1, 200–2
    social skills training 36, 98–111, 202–7

verbalization in learning situations 35
thimerosal (mercury-based immunization
    preservative) 19
tidiness, teaching organizational skills 161–3
"time out" sessions 47
toileting problems, withholding bowel movements
    156–8
toys, and fixations 75–7
"transitioning" difficulties 21
treatment options see therapeutic interventions

uncooperative behaviors 87–8

verbal abilities see language abilities
verbal "labeling" 22, 35, 160
    and lack of discovery learning abilities 24–5,
        33–4, 160–1
visual-spatial (organizational) disorders
    causes 17–18
    manifestations and signs 21–2, 34, 161–3
vocabulary 128
    see also language abilities

walking/hiking 113–14
washing up 162–3
websites 215–16
    Family Communications, Inc. (FCI) 148
    peer support for LD children 193
    Special Education Law 193
"White Matter Model" (Rourke) 17–18
writing abilities 128
    alternatives for NLD children 35
    observations and signs of NLD 26